regime 04

a magazine of new writing

regime
books

Regime 04: A Magazine of New Writing
Contributing Editor: Andrew Burke
Editors: Nathan Hondros (Poetry) and Damon Lockwood (Short Stories)
Editorial Assistant: Michelle Espinoza

Published by Regime Books in Australia, 2014.
First Floor, 456 William Street, Perth.
www.regimebooks.com.au
www.twitter.com/regimebooks
www.instagram.com/regimebooks

Copyright remains with the authors, who assert all rights in relation to their work.

Cover image:
Jacqueline Ball, *Subcompact #3 (detail)*
(2014, archival inkjet print on photo rag, 78 x 110cm)
© Jacqueline Ball — www.jacquelineball.com

With thanks to our supporters:

    Jim Davis
    John and Jan Hondros
    Turner Galleries (www.turnergalleries.com.au)

ISBN 978-0-9874821-3-6
ISSN 2200-7822

CONTENTS

Poetry

Susan Adams	Puppet On A Wire	47
Jeffrey Alfier	Farm Girl Harvesting Ryegrass at Sixmilecross	66
Stuart Barnes	Elementals	14
	Forcento	16
Andrew Bifield	The Car Will Not Start	50
	August, 2013	51
Ahimsa Timoteo Bodhrán	Nueva York/Lenapehoking	36
Andrew Burke	On the Verge	2
	Stories	1
Ashley Capes	Thunderclap	52
Sue Clennell	The Maidens of Artemis	69
Robbie Coburn	To Madelaine	40
	The Invisible Sister	41
Melissah Comber	Airport, 6AM	19
Raven Current	In Someone Else's Words	100
Jim Davis	Future Lemons	65
Ivan de Monbrison	Untitled	82
	The Night	84
Colin Dodds	Not Just Stars	87
Á. N. Dvořák	The Ruin	49
Phillip A. Ellis	For Stuart Barnes	105
Aaron Furnell	Home Truths	81
Mike Greenacre	Preston Point	70
Stu Hatton	vectors	63
Kenneth Hudson	My Front Verandah	88
Ross Jackson	Castrado	99
Helga Jermy	Sudden Shower over Ulverstone Bridge	46
Vasiliki Katsarou	Cycladia	10
Winifred Kavalieris	psych hospital	21
Richard King Perkins II	Diary of a Sensitive Youth	97
Christopher Konrad	Seidel doesn't care (ad honorem)	96
Roland Leach	My Father's Country	17
Cameron Lowe	The Lilies	103
	A New Room for Spring	104
Bruce McRae	Forgotten Promise	102
Dean Meredith	How to Spot a Pervert	53
Karla Linn Merrifield	Aubade in Nine Amphibrachs	67
Carly-Jay Metcalfe	Primitive	4
Jan Napier	Reframing Frieda	62

Poetry (Continued)

Allan Padgett	*I Dream of Jeannie*	73
Geoff Page	*Ruling the Waves*	6
Vanessa Page	*Maranoa*	86
Carl Palmer	*Senior Moment*	91
Mark Roberts	*prehistory*	48
Mather Schneider	*Almost Everything*	106
Michele Seminara	*my ekphrasis is a fraud*	12
	The Lover	13
Barnaby Smith	*Beach Suburb*	20
Ian C. Smith	*Alison Long Ago*	61
Ashleigh Synnott	*Plumb Thumb*	54
Roger Vickery	*Family Court Orders*	90
Ben Walter	*The Rock*	89

Interview

	Jacqueline Ball: Bone and Muscle, Force and Restraint	30

Fiction

Libbie Chellew		
Christopher Konrad	*Early Signs*	92
Stephen Pollock	*Rene T and Dog Investigations*	55
Deborah Sheldon	*Weltschmerz*	75
Danielle Spinks	*Broken Things*	24
	The Benley Acquisition	108

Notes on Contributors

122

Andrew Burke

Stories

        he tells her
                like fish to burly
in a vacant lot   a gum leaf in white knickers
                on the back seat

                      a recognised cliché
                        ocean waves as she breaks

        she is   smoking moonlight

cheapness when you look
                rolling out his tongue
        like the ocean   he wraps his tale around her
                                'Wait
                              No tidy endings'
                she says that cheapens it
laughs again, seriously
narratively

                he must be having her on
                        ocean air complete with
      one-legged seagulls in summer

                late train catches his ear
          whistling through the preface

On the Verge

out early
watering the roses
before sunrise

I scratch my neck
and dislodge a bee

drunk already

~

next week's
council pick-up
has grown a fair crop

fringing the road
on browning grass

white goods
stained lounges

broken bikes and
office chairs that don't
hold office anymore

~

when evening falls
young boys

punch the shit out of
the washing machine
which once washed
their nappies

leaving the white pedestal
standing
        arse up

~

all creatures have
Buddha-nature

except bored boys*

*with apologies to Gary Snyder

Carly-Jay Metcalfe

Primitive

Gun empty, shot with intent
I hoof hit/wheel roll/foot fall
dropping girasol like unfolding lies
then wait with convivial pause.
In the morning, a thump over the cattle grate;
the scene of an arrival; a foal on the run, mourning mothers milk.

In the night-time
we're running moonshine over state lines,
black boot mafia
crossing chain link fences 'til
we're making diamonds outta prayers.
Mouth raging pink with sainfoin,
dog soldiers lean on mud-brown huts — sharply muscled,
diesel in their veins and peach faced fuzz.

With the fleeting glare of a fox, I cut my teeth on the mountains
of my girlhood, for some pernicious reward that never came,
but through ravens call, hearken this…
ancestral voices dampen the well,
carrying my body boat in their fallacious swell.
Your tears collect in the hollow of my spine
so I stay stilled 'til they are dried.

A film of your despair visible only by the rush of midnight
and only one minute at that.
Thrown from your skin,
bones akimbo to the wind.
Death an internship,
slicing away at dreams and blanketed forces of thought.

A stretch of joy and a garrote of light;
action put to the sword after a night of liberty.
Beauty is perilous, from cradle to casket *(you should know this by now)*
Unfold your eyes to the timbre of salute.
Peel open your mouth to speak a salacious moot of sin;
unknotting your limbs from unfeeling,
digging your fingers into the loam,
'cos your daddy said, 'there's honey in that soil, milk in them stones.'

Seeking out the ground with eyes I put to sleep so many years ago,
I kneel and pat away at moistening roly-poly roots —
the pads of my fingers dewy and yielding
stamped with flecks of broken china
from seventeen nights of rain.
In the morning, we roll through doorjambs.
You walk behind me; I am your windbreaker.
How many accidents until we collide?

For there is a necklace of deep regret that won't come loose —
la douleur exquise —
there is nothing ordinary about this.

Eating from the hands of the land,
summer steals in, tearing winter away.
The blood red of birth, the placenta of earth
that cannot be washed away.

Geoff Page

Ruling the Waves

The first book I remember clearly
reading on my own
was called **Highroads of History**
(Nelson, 1945).
I took a chapter every morning
in bed before I went to school
while boarding with my aunt and uncle
in town when I was eight.
My mother, who had earlier
overseen my two slow years
of school by correspondence,
tracked it down for me in Sydney,
three volumes, all in all,
a greeny sort of canvas binding,
the author modestly unnamed,
all three books designed to hymn
our Empire recently preserved —
though India the year before
had slipped off unobserved.
I also failed to notice then
that Volume III was dated
1943.
A foreword promised me in rhyme:
Little children in these pages
You shall learn the tale of ages;
You shall learn the wondrous story
Of our Britain's fame and glory.
The font was large, Times Roman.
The paragraphs were numbered

for classroom reference.
The text was based on 'famous paintings',
notable events and persons.
The men were 'gallant' mostly;
'upright', 'stout' or 'sturdy'
if sourced from lower down.
The women were unfailingly
'gentle', 'kind' and 'true'
except perhaps for bad Queen Mary.
Romans, Angles, Danes and Normans
crossing in their turn
were met with 'valiant' resistance —
vide 'Hereward the Wake',
master of the marshes.
Those Vikings, too, who challenged Harold.
'Arriving in three hundred ships,
they fled in twenty-four'.
The English had, in Volume II,
with Augustine presiding,
converted to the 'one true God'.
Chronology was not the point:
King Arthur with his circled knights;
King Alfred, prone to burning cakes;
Robin Hood in Sherwood Forest
shifting in and out of myth.
Jousts between the Roses flourished
alternately in White and Red
before the Tudors and the Stuarts.
Kings from time to time were 'slain'
(it sounded fairly painless)
for favouring their 'favourites'
or being too much given to
their taste for 'wicked pleasures'.
Century by century
our Empire had expanded
courtesy mild-mannered gents
like Clive of India, James Wolfe
and Captain Cook from Whitby.
Occasionally, when ill-advised,

'cruel natives' were inclined to rise
against their 'British masters'.
Each volume had the same great sweep
with extras added in.
Volume III had twenty pages
printed twice — and twenty pages
missing. I've noticed this just now,
reading it straight through again
sixty-six years later.
How is it that I have them still
and almost nothing else
surviving from that year in town?
There is some scribble here and there
added by a sibling
who, seemingly, was unpersuaded.
My mother must have kept them for me,
knowing I would need them later.
It's possible I never reached
the heights of Volume III,
aged eight and forty miles from home
week by week by week.
Unknown to me, our Empire
even then was cracking.
Each morning was, however, still
a coronation march,
the generals and admirals,
the golden kings and queens
the doublets with their lordly reds
and silver sleeves of ermine,
the ensigns raised with puff of smoke,
the buccaneers like Drake and Raleigh
but also the improvers:
Wilberforce who freed the slaves;
the saintly Florence Nightingale
redeeming the Crimea.
My mother truly loved the British
and, though she had no time for heaven,
this stained-glass version slanted down,
enriched with scarlets, blues and purples.

It underwrote the future.
She tried so hard when I was eight
to hand it on to me.
Almost successfully.

Vasiliki Katsarou

Cycladia

1.

Slim round pastel
Cycladic stones

I turn over
in my palm

as the sun darkens
me to the shade
of pale wood

2.

I found a knucklebone
sea pebble chiseled by time
into die

I found a cuttlefish bone
ovoid obole
stone almost
balsa wood

Coins of no realm
cast ashore

scoured of their stamps
eyed and palmed

awaiting traces
of us

3.

Sifnos means empty
le gouffre, quoi

Each terrassed hill —
pyramidal —
an inverse vessel

us through time
from Iron Age to plastics

and this graffitied amphora
a cipher of modernity

4.

Cuttlefish bone, sea stone
to remind us that history

is leaving your marks
before the obole arrives

obsolete
at its destination

Michele Seminara

my ekphrasis is a fraud

hands
hard
on the head of the stick
shoved into his mouth
to choke violent eruptions

eyes
crazed horses
restrained beneath
brows of extreme malcontent

she
with her handkerchief
twisting and twisting
a noose around the wrist
of despair's swollen neck

this is the picture I used to mask our love's lament

*Inspired by Scottish artist Thomas Faed's painting of a miserable couple, entitled 'Faults on Both Sides'.

The Lover

The skin's sumptuously soft.   The body's thin,
               hairless,

                       vulnerable. She doesn't look
       She   Touches   his
sex,   caresses   the strange
novelty. He moans,   In dreadful love

And   the pain is
slowly   borne towards pleasure.

Stuart Barnes

Elementals

Who are these people at the bridge to meet me? They are the villagers —
Two. Of course there are two.
First, are you our sort of person?
The word of a snail on the plate of a leaf?
What was she doing when it blew in

What is this, behind this veil, is it ugly, is it beautiful?
The courage of the shut mouth, in spite of artillery!
This is the light of the mind, cold and planetary.
My night sweats grease his breakfast plate.
Empty, I echo to the least footfall,

I know the bottom, she says. I know it with my great tap root:
The abstracts hover like dull angels:
Stasis in darkness.
A secret! A secret!
I ordered this, this clean wood box

What a thrill —
Bare-handed, I hand the combs.
Clownlike, happiest on your hands,
Love set you going like a fat gold watch.
Love, the world

A squeal of brakes.
Viciousness in the kitchen!
This is the sea, then, this great abeyance.
Off that landspit of stony mouth-plugs,

Over your body the clouds go

Pure? What does it mean?
The tulips are too excitable, it is winter here.
Even the sun-clouds this morning cannot manage such skirts.
Somebody is shooting at something in our town —
It was a place of force —

A smile fell in the grass.
O half moon —
Jade —
If the moon smiled, she would resemble you.
You come in late, wiping your lips.

No use, no use, now, begging Recognize.
I am a miner. The light burns blue.
How far is it?
I have done it again.
You do not do, you do not do

This is the easy time, there is nothing doing.

A cento sourced from Sylvia Plath's Ariel: The Restored Edition.

Forcento

It's gravity, spilling in capillaries, cheek-tissue trembling,
oozing past gravity to snuggle
Anne's rose-sweet gravity, and the stiff grave

I would admire the deep gravity of it, its tireless eyes.
But Gravity — and Expectation — and Fear —
and gravity, scientists say, is weak.

A cento sourced from Anne Winters' 'The Mill-Race', Anne Sexton's 'Venus and the Ark', Margaret Avison's 'New Year's Poem', Sylvia Plath's 'A Birthday Present', Emily Dickinson's 'Unit, like Death, for Whom?', Jane Hirshfield's 'For What Binds Us'.

Roland Leach

My Father's Country

My father dreamed of heading back to the bush,
as if he'd turn into some former self that he was pleased to live with,
as if a turn off the road would have done it all for him,
given back what that bitch life had tricked him out of.
But I don't hear all these stories till later when he's half-gone
with dementia, looking grey and dribbling white lizards of saliva,
and he tells me about his best roo-dog slit from throat to arse by the claws
of some big roo. He had kneeled next to the dog as he stitched him
up with a chaff-bag needle and fishing line. He would say,
 'me old dad taught us boys to be men, we'd never go without food
if we ever got lost', and I'm thinking he's lost now on this small bed,
lost on this 6 by 3 softness, but he makes me shake his hand as I leave,
gripping it like it doesn't matter if it kills him,
showing he's still a man even after the prostate op and the incontinence.

By his bedside I think that it would have been better had he died
years ago, maybe propped up at the bar at the Castle,
or even a honourable heart-attack in a brawl, like he belonged
to one of those tribes that had to be beaten to death when its darkness approached,
dying with his fists raised so evil spirits wouldn't escape with his weakened soul. He
would have liked it that way, knowing the mortician had to fix him up as if he was a
cuts-doctor at the side of a boxing ring, it would be a man's death,
not the propped up remains who looks out the window at roses and jacarandas,
the family coming to see him, all saying feeling better dad?

Perhaps Saturday arvos aren't too bad for him, like they always have been.
He's seated up in a chair and my sister and husband are leaning forward
on the bed watching tv and Yippyio has just won the Derby and some mad punter
had lost a hundred grand on Marble Halls who had just gone down by a head,

and now there's the footy and Geelong & the Eagles are fighting out a thriller,
Benny Cousin's just got one in the eye and it's closed up already,
and maybe for a hour the blood is pumping again, the aching knee joints
are forgotten and he might be thinking that's it's alright leaving the fights
to the younger blokes, knowing that with all their injuries they're not going
to be any better when they're 78, and in the end there's not much you can do about it.

Melissah Comber

Airport, 6AM

emerge from recirculated air
        take off layers
          reassemble hair
place skin in storage compartments.

Outside:
The scent of jacarandas permeates the humidity.

I tell you nothing can compare to this:
With a pointed look, you say you can think of a few things.

Inside:
Good espresso coffee and feeling of contentment that polarises and stuns.

Outside:
Cicada cacophony and chirping sweat.

I tell you nothing can compare to this.
You tell me it is overcast.
I say that I don't care, because I know the sun is still there.

In the car you turn up the radio and recirculated air.

Barnaby Smith

Beach Suburb

this square mile is not Tangiers though
one is still afflicted by all the different
types of shoes in an international zone

                                      boundaries widened by accession and
                                      potted with lovingly crafted funerals at
                                      each dusk determining there is no such
                                      thing as the voyage home

symmetrical symphonies of housing
glazed venereal and overstated half-
truths the glue between friends graffiti
artists the city's great celebrants pad lightly
in local vinegary air

                                      from the kerb an open terrace door
                                      and a woman hunched breastfeeding
                                      inside a cave a baby with lungs bigger
                                      than all things

with shapes in his head colliding and
crashing those puddingy limbs won't
fight more a lament for this season's
harvest of half-eaten bodies on the
street and on the sand

Winifred Kavalieris

psych hospital

1
she's sitting with the others around a table
scissors glue womens weekly house and
garden new idea steve gives each an empty notebook to
fill with pictures and words

john is crying at the end
of the table

today she can't she
   can't
          pick
      up
            the
                scissors

2
mike's staring at the lump of
white play dough in his hand
he looks mad
julie the nice nurse asks
what are you going to make mike
what are you going to make
mike gets really mad and
yells this is it

3
it's morning group they're sitting in a circle
no body wants to do the jobs they all wait and wait
no one looks at any one so she starts to write names on the jobs list
feed fish sue lunch dave water plants jane
the marker is black and it's nearly run out
the whiteboard is smudgy
her hand is shaky
she was   a   teacher

4
jane's on fire she went out for a smoke and came back up three flights of
stairs with ash burning in one cuff of her jeans I'm on fire she giggled
and steve the nurse ran and put her out

5
gloria is new
she tells them her baby died
and she wants to kill herself
she plays the guitar that's got one string missing
and she sings
she sings and laughs
wears a hot pink t-shirt that says
honey I'm a lesbian
one day she screams and screams
and a nurse takes her to the quiet room
we don't see gloria the next day
or ever again
gloria's bracelet had tiny
tinkling silver bells
gloria

6
every lunch time they queue
for corned beef salad bread and
every lunch time they struggle to get

one hand into one regulation
hygienic plastic glove

it's a test she says
the three-second test
when you pass you're ready
to be discharged

7
wish I could wave a magic wand and
make you better the nurses always said

on the day she's discharged
she gives the group a clear plastic magic
wand with silver and gold and red sparkling
stars floating inside it and a pair of dress-up
glasses that make you see rainbows everywhere
and a notebook filled with pictures

Deborah Sheldon

Broken Things

The weatherboard bungalow was built into a hillside. Craig, on crutches, had to negotiate the steep asphalt path from the carport to the front door. Dad trotted down the slope with their suitcases, and then strolled back up a minute later to put his hands on his hips and shake his head over Craig's slow descent. Dad's scrutiny made Craig feel like a kid again instead of a man in his twenties, and the feeling irritated him.

At last, Craig stood inside the old house. The kitchen was unchanged as far as he could remember, except for a fish tank the size of a wide-screen TV that sat on a cabinet near the back door. Craig used his good foot to drag out a chair from the kitchen table.

Dad said, 'Bet you never pictured being under my roof again.'

Craig lowered himself into the chair and said, 'Where do you want these?'

Dad took the crutches and propped them against the wall nearest the tank. Two angelfish darted from the greenery and flitted against the glass with the intensity of moths hammering a bright window.

Dad laughed. 'See that, mate? Reckon they missed me or what?'

Dad squatted in front of the tank, his nose at the glass. More fish rose from hidden places in dark foliage. Craig looked at the flashes of colours, stripes and scales, but mostly looked at Dad. He had aged plenty. The chapped, whiskery skin hung from his face as if his skull had shrunk. They hadn't seen each other in eleven years. The car trip from the hospital in Adelaide to this house on Melbourne's outskirts had taken the best part of a day, and yet they'd hardly spoken. Well, Craig thought, some things don't change. Then he said, 'I didn't know you liked fish.'

The doorbell sounded.

Dad checked his watch. 'That'll be Amy. She must've been watching for the car.'

'Amy?'

Dad headed to the front door. 'The foster kid from over the road. She's at my aquarist hobby group. A good kid, you'll like her.'

'What hobby group? Dad? Don't let her in.'

Craig pressed his fingertips into his eye sockets. The world burst into red blotches. When he opened his eyes again, he saw a thin girl of about twelve standing at the fish tank with her back to him. She wore a grey school uniform. Her lank home-cut hair was the colour of cheese.

'You better check ammonia and nitrite,' she said to Dad. 'A storm a couple a days ago knocked out the power. We only got it back this morning.'

Dad made an exasperated sound. 'Christ, that'd be right. Gone for just two bloody days, now look at Sweetie's tail, would you? She's got it clamped.' He flung open the doors of the cabinet below the tank and took out a box. The box held white plastic bottles and test tubes.

'I'll do ammonia,' Amy said, and turned to grab one of the bottles. Craig noticed that her eyes were blue and recalled those other blue eyes: those round and startled ones.

'Dad,' Craig said, 'my crutches.'

'Here you go, mate.'

Craig left the kitchen. It was quiet in the lounge room. He half-sat, half-lay across the couch and listened to the ticking of the wall clock. Amy came in after a while and squatted next to him. She gave off a sour loamy smell like wet dirt. She rested her hand on his cast.

'Don't touch it,' he said.

'I broke my arm once; crashed my scooter into a wall.'

'Move your hand.'

Amy stood up. 'I've still got the cast, everybody signed it. Why hasn't anybody signed yours?'

He turned his face and closed his eyes. When he at last looked around, Amy was gone. He could hear the clock but couldn't see it. The shadows in the lounge room had deepened and were pushing against him.

'Dad,' he called out.

Dad came in, wiping his hands on a towel. 'We got to get to the aquarium shop before it shuts. Come on, I'm not leaving you to mope.'

The aquarium shop was long and narrow. Lighted tanks lay along both walls. The tanks, burbling and droning, were full of dark shapes. Craig stayed by the front door and leaned on his crutches, breathing hard, while the cast dragged on him like a shark trying to pull him under.

After a few minutes, Dad emerged from an aisle with a teenaged boy. The suggestion of a goatee beard struggled from the boy's chin. Half his work-shirt hung loose from his trousers like he didn't care for the job anyway and his lopsided nametag announced him as Toby, Fish World Customer Consultant.

'This is my son, Craig,' Dad said.

'Yeah?' Toby said.

'He has to stay with me for a while. Road accident.'

'Really?' Toby said and winked at Craig.

'You don't know the half of it,' Dad said. 'Busted nearly every bone in his body, didn't you mate? Riding his motorbike, minding his own business, and t-boned a woman coming out of a side street. Bang.' Dad speared his hand flat through the air and whistled to demonstrate Craig's trajectory. 'Straight over the top of her car.'

And hit the road like a stone skipping across water, Craig thought. Bounce, bounce, bounce, then stillness, three-quarter moon coolly overhead, sirens.

'Wow,' Toby said and grinned.

Back in Dad's kitchen, Craig sat at the table while Dad siphoned water from the fish tank into a sixty-litre plastic drum. The water level fell away and plants sucked their leaves against the glass. Dad had bought a bottle from the aquarium shop and Craig picked it up from the table and read the packaging. *Releases vast quantities of nitrifying bacteria into the water to reduce the risk of fish loss.* Craig put down the bottle and said, 'Toby's an arsehole.'

'He knows his fish.'

'Yeah, well, he's still an arsehole.'

'I've already told you once. Now don't start with me, by God.'

'Okay, okay, forget it.' Then Craig said, 'I'm gonna go home anyway.'

'To Adelaide? Ha! What for? You can't teach at the karate club so how do you plan on earning a wage and paying your rent? You don't even have a car and even if you did, how the blazes are you gonna drive it with your leg the way it is? And not one of your so-called mates gives a rat's. So where does that leave you? Exactly nowhere but here, and don't think I like it any better than you do.'

Craig clamped his jaw and, despite himself, recalled the physiotherapist from his two months in hospital; Millie, the bitch with the doughy face and fat, callused hands. She had come to his ward every day to make him wave his arms, touch his toes and squeeze a tennis ball, goading him to stand and walk and stretch and strive and he had hated her and her loud, relentless cheeriness. Throughout every painful exercise he had insisted that, given time, he would recover like nothing had ever happened and go back to karate, weights and running while Millie doggedly maintained that some things, once broken, could never heal and he was one of them. Now he understood what she had meant. He understood so well, so completely, that it weighted his guts.

Craig said, 'I'll catch a train home on Monday.'

Dad, who had been lugging the sixty-litre drum to the kitchen sink, thumped the drum to floor. 'Yeah? And then what? Live on the streets like a bum? Now give me a bloody hand with this water change.'

That night, Craig went to bed in his old room. The wooden bed-head still bore gummy traces of the dinosaur stickers that he'd applied some twenty years ago and the familiar paint chips in the wall next to his pillow disturbed him. With his eyes shut tight he was seven again, the bright kid who had a knack for sports and a mother who loved him and was still alive. He fell asleep imagining her cool hand on his forehead and his future beckoning large and sure. Then he woke up, a figure looming over him.

'You were yelling,' Dad said. He was wearing pyjama bottoms and nothing else, his chest flabby as if someone had let out the air.

Craig said. 'Get out of here, let me sleep.'

Dad left the room and shut the door. Craig fell back onto the bed. His leg rang with a clenched ache that never stopped no matter how many pills he swallowed. He blamed it on the bone tissue forced to grow torturously like a vine around the screws, bolts and wires that held his leg together. But sometimes, like now, he recognised the pain as the phantom wail of his kneecap that had shattered so thoroughly that the surgeon had simply given up on it and tossed every last little fragment – more than sixty in all, according to a theatre nurse – into a medical waste bin.

He got up. In the kitchen, he closed the door to the hallway and switched on the tank lights. Fish stirred out of plants and rose from the gravel, coasting in the warm water. Craig got a chair and sat down. A silver angelfish, no bigger than a ten-cent coin, struggled past, its tail furled to a point instead of fanned like the other fish. It swam back and forth in a hitching motion and gulped strenuously at the water.

The hall door opened. Dad sat down at the table.

Craig pointed at the tank. 'Is that Sweetie, the one with the tail? What's wrong with her?'

'Poisoned. The blackout stopped the pump. That dropped the oxygen in the water and killed off the good bacteria.'

Craig didn't understand, but let it go. 'The other fish seem okay.'

'They're bigger. They've got what's known as constitution.' Then Dad said, 'It's three in the morning, mate.'

'I keep seeing her eyes. Just before I hit her door, she looked at me.'

Dad got up, reached over the hood of the tank and switched off the lights. Sweetie disappeared into the sudden black.

After breakfast, Craig sat at the table with coffee while Dad prepared another water change for the fish tank. He put the sixty-litre drum and siphon on the kitchen floor, opened the lid of the tank and said through his teeth, 'Bugger it.'

'Is she dead?'

'Near enough.'

Craig grabbed his crutches and stumped over to the tank. Sweetie was bobbing in the gentle current on her side, fins slack, wide eyes clouded.

'Blast it. Come here, Sweetie.' Dad slid his hand into the tank and scooped her out. The fish lay motionless in Dad's palm, glossy as a drop of sap. Craig went out the backdoor to the balcony, took a seat on one of the benches and leaned against the house.

The yard below was a sea of eucalyptus trees. A stiff wind shimmered at millions of wet leaves. The rain came and went and came again. Then Amy was on the balcony and glaring at him, her squinty eyes red-rimmed.

'What?' he snapped.

'Nothing. Sweetie's dead. You don't even care.'

'Shouldn't you be at school?'

'It's Saturday.'

Craig sat up and said, 'Jesus, why are you always here? Haven't you got somewhere to go?'

She kicked a sneaker-shod foot at his cast, too far away to connect, but before he could stop himself, Craig flinched and jarred his knee. Crackles of white pain sliced through his leg and bit into his ankle. The agony concussed in waves, yet he was aware of Amy observing him, unmoved. As soon as he was able, he grabbed a crutch and swung it. Amy skipped out of the way.

He blushed and hurled the crutch to the balcony floor. 'Piss off.'

'You piss off, you cripple.' Sneering, she hissed, 'You murderer.'

Craig's heart dropped, swung and clattered against his ribs. He finally said, 'She ran the stop sign, not me.'

'So what. She had a baby in the back, didn't she? Now it's got to grow up without a mum.' Amy's face collapsed for a moment into a sobbing grimace. Then she set her jaw and stabbed a middle finger at him. He struggled to stand up, lunging for his crutches, but she had already slammed the backdoor behind her.

When he finished crying, Craig slid off the chair, bore his weight on his good leg and leaned over to gather both crutches. It took him some time to descend the balcony's slick wooden steps. At last he stood on the foaming wet mush of the backyard. Rain peppered his face and weighted his jumper. He picked his way through the trees down to the rear of the backyard. Over a low chicken-wire fence ploughed the brown murmur of the Yarra River, its surface jumping with countless strikes of rain. He stepped over the fence.

The cold water poured into his cast and soothed his skin. The relief urged him to stride further into the flow. When the river was waist-high, he allowed it to wrench the crutches from his grip and hurl them out of sight. Wading was difficult now without the crutches to stabilise him. He took a couple more steps. The river pushed him over and swirled him in circles, dunking him, pitching him downstream so fast that Dad's backyard flurried out of sight in an instant, gone forever.

Tearing along felt like a thrilling ride until the plaster cast, heavy and sodden, pulled him under. The river drove itself into his nose and throat. It occurred to him that he didn't have the strength to make it to the bank, even if salvation was what he wanted. The horror of it made him thrash and shriek for a few seconds until he could steel himself. He clumsily flipped onto his back, spitting river. Branches flashed by overhead. The rushing water cradled him. Sticks and leaves churned furiously alongside as if racing him to the finish line, but he knew he would get there first.

The blue eyes came to mind. He apologised again for the millionth time. This time his apology would really mean something.

An Interview with Jacqueline Ball

Bone and Muscle, Force and Restraint

For a young artist who's only been at the forefront of her field a handful of years, Jacqueline Ball's photography reveals an astonishing emotional maturity that is pushing the boundaries of her medium. Her photography is at once sophisticated and suggestive, understated and physically powerful. Regime Books was lucky enough to have a preview of Jacqueline's work that Turner Galleries will be exhibiting as part of the Melbourne Art Fair in August.

This new work extends what seems to be a fascination with challenging the ideas of portraiture and the representation of landscape; bodies are examined as though they are part of the natural world. Jacqueline's work distorts your sense of scale. You know you're staring at flesh, but at times you can trick yourself into thinking you're looking at a landscape. These were just our first thoughts. It turns out that there is so much more to Jacqueline's work.

As we're always rediscovering, your Regime correspondents are dilletantes of the visual arts. We know what moves us, and we know groundbreaking and exciting art when we see it. Jacqueline Ball's work is all these things; we sat down with her over a beer to find out exactly why.

Jacqueline, can you tell us when you were first hit by the compulsion to make art? How old were you? Did it seem natural? Was it someone else's artwork that you saw and fell in love with that first sparked the notion?

There was no single, intense moment of compulsion. It was more like a gradual progression. However, I did want to be an artist as a child, with barely any knowledge of what it entailed. I also wanted to be a swimmer, a filmmaker and a musician. Still, while it was a gradual move towards being an artist, it certainty wasn't a passive or accidental inclination. I considered a number of other careers in various creative industries. Your use of the word 'natural' to me suggests a degree of ease and comfort of sliding into it. For me, though, discomfort and anxiety are vital forces in my decision. As such, it has always been important to continually reflect on my decision to make stuff. After my first year at art school I was left feeling disillusioned and took the following year off. When I went back after my break it was with a renewed intensity. A kind of obsessiveness emerged. And now I understand that there needs to be some sort of force within me to bother doing it. Anyway, right now the ideas, or energies, of force and propulsion have recently been at the forefront of my thinking and they're contributing to the current shifts in my practice.

You mention a shift in your practice towards force and propulsion, (which is fascinating; more questions later), but I just wanted to ask about the work that's led you to this point. Prior to this new work, you seem to mess with distortions of scale. The size of your photographic reproductions can be enormous, but the scale of your subjects isn't always clear. When I look at your work, I love that I'm not always sure whether I'm seeing a detail of person, or a sculpture, or a landscape. Can you talk about how this came to interest you?

Photographs always incorporate some ambiguity due to the nature of the camera as recording device and like many others, I'm interested in how I can utilize this ambiguity to mediate the subject matter. For me this is focused on documenting the progressions of the sculptural objects (or body) as I erase, construct and reconfigure them. It's like building up layers in three dimensions for the sole purpose of making them flat. I enjoy observing the weird translations that occur between the object and its representation and I've been interested in this since I started taking photos as a teenager. Shifting from a documentary approach to studio based constructed images gave me more control to enhance the weird translations. So I'm always aware that the lens inevitably distorts. I can use a limited depth of field and specific lens to further emphasize this. I can apply light to the subject to manipulate the content, exposing and concealing particularities. I can build structures that are warped even before being photographed and I can make materials look as if they are made from something other than what they are.

    I also think a lot about how I want people to orientate themselves in relation to scale and content and how to create images that destabilize. Prompting connections between the body of the viewer and image is one of the central drives for printing at a large scale. For example, the work I made for *Primavera* at the Museum of Contemporary Art last year was eight large images (overall the work was 4.3m x 5.9m in size) that at close proximity fill your field of vision, perhaps dwarfing the body through the scale of the double hang. The presence of weighted forms suspended above your head and the fleshy repositories that are of bodily proportion try to connect the work back to a physicality. The large scale and high placement also introduces distortion through perspective shifts.

    In relation to references within the content, I'm interested in how associations accumulate. I'm trying to find spaces that are in-between things, slippery and in motion. I'm hoping this mesh of connections allows room for things to fall from other things.

And, finally, in terms of my general approach, I know this all sounds very planned out but I actually swing between meticulous, methodical processes and intuitive modes of working.

Your new work is full of the idea of force, but also restraint (for example skin bound with rope). Can you tell us how this came to interest you? And could you talk about the counterbalance between force and restraint?

I don't think there can be force without constraint as it is constraint that gives force its value. There are always oppositional references within my images. I'm approaching these opposites as 'different aspects of the same thing, inseparable from each other'[1], to refer to Elizabeth Grosz. I think force and restraint has always been of interest through how I modulate boundaries. When making images that are structured like a portal, I'm setting up a contained space with perimeters. I can connect this to the idea of compression, claustrophobia, directional movement all of which can suggest a force. When arranging the body, the sections form edges. Bone, muscle, fat and skin puts pressure on other bits of bone, muscle, fat and skin. Objects are pushed up against this too. I'm recording actual physicality between my partner and I, moments of closeness. The gestures/actions are rendered static. Skin acts as material and its damage communicates its permeability. Rope and fabric contain bits of body and prompt immobility. I think a lot of about accumulation here, of every element adding to every other element.

However in saying all this, I don't know if my work is actually forceful and I always want it to be more than what it is. Sometimes I think the force is present in the space the work is coming from, rather than what the images are actually doing. I'm trying not to mythologise my images, but I do I have desire for intense, emotional force of some sort and my recent work in particular is coming out of this. I wonder how much of this is actually evidenced in the image and sometimes I get obsessed with predicting viewer's subjective responses. The grounding space I come back to is a desire to create image fragments that come from a charged space and that are suggestive rather than illustrative.

As a creative artist, the obsession interests us, and we share it in our own work. Have you thought about where it comes from with you? What is it that stokes the fire?

At the moment I'm really into the idea of framing everything I do as problem

---

[1] Elizabeth A. Grosz, *Volatile Bodies: Toward a Corporeal Feminism*, 2004, page 11.

solving. I'm obsessive with falling hard into my work, when you feel like you are almost at something good and everything around you drops away. There is the stress and anxiety that is the counter to this, but I'm learning to use those states too. Once the series is completed, and often after some time has passed, I then see a new set of problems. These gaps prompt a need for new solutions. I really dig this cycle. It's full of propulsion, movement and growth.

Can you tell us about some of the artists, contemporary or otherwise, that have influenced your work? Was there a piece that you saw and which inspired you after your year of disillusion?

There was no particular piece of work that shifted things for me during that time. In undergrad I was obsessed with artists like Robert Rauschenberg, Bill Henson, Pat Brassington, Bill Viola, Thomas Demand, James Turrell and Wolfgang Tillmans. More recently artists such as Sakia Olde Wolbers, Paul Knight, Max Pam, Hans Bellmer, Roger Ballen have been important. The most profound gallery experiences I've had have been surprise moments that are charged and intense, a kind of sensory shock that is felt in the body. It's particularly interesting when the specifics of the artist don't take over and it's really just about being in the presence of the work. I think what happened is that I was suddenly more open to that 'liveness' after coming back to study.

Is it possible to separate art from life? Can you walk into the studio and leave everything at the door?

Deliberately or not, everything I make is inherently biographical to some degree. I think my awareness of this connect has become more evident in the past six months and this has in turn contributed to less compartmentalisation and for my 'studio life' and 'everything else life' to connect with more fluidity. For example, I'm now making work at home, work that is immediate, responsive and documentary, and I'm regularly taking photos in my everyday. There is a long history to draw from of photographers merging practice and life. Still, it is a new space to navigate, and the shift feels authentic and truly important to me.

When Allison from Turner Galleries first showed us your new work, we were really struck by the flesh tones, and the shadows. I can see, but not quite describe, that there is something very erotic going on there. Any chance we can convince you to talk about that?

I think about erotics as a mode of connection, a pathway through the world that is not necessarily about sex. Where I am with this is on the side of Deleuze where desire is about producing new forms, though I should say my understanding of the theory of all this is still quite rudimentary.

Anyway, I think my old work did make some suggestion to the body and erotics. For example creating objects spotlit for display, with seductive surfaces, tube-like orifices etc. It's just that this interest has incrementally increased and gotten more obvious as a result. More recently, I've been thinking about building works that are honest, more personal expressions about intense and intimate shared experiences. I'm trying not to illustrate any kind of erotics, but rather I am interested in physicality and its codes and the way it moves and intersects with our seeing.

This has come out of a degree of rediscovery of my attitudes to body in general, a lot of which has been about learning about the grammar of the representation of male sexuality/visuality. I'm increasingly interested in the male body as softened, damaged and exposed. This doesn't come from a feminist impulse to turn the tables; it's more about beauty, finding power in vulnerability, transcending binaries and finding new ways to think about gendered physicality and desire. It's coming at the male body from a place that is not embedded with patriarchal or phallocentric structures of sexuality. But, I'm really just working through these ideas at the moment; there are many uncertainties and aspects I don't yet fully understand.

I read about your residencies in Iceland and Finland (in 2011). Iceland, especially, is renowned for its landscapes. I wonder how time in those countries (ones I'd love to visit) influenced your work?

Back then I was really interested in spending time in spaces that represented the opposite of suburban Perth. I had this strong desire for immersion and the experience of being overwhelmed by the unfamiliar. Natural formations, isolation, old world expeditions and disintegration were some of the things I researched. Then, as you say, there was also a fixation on intense experience in landscape, feeling vulnerable and insignificant in relation to monumental structures that almost invade your field of vision, as well as the often threatening experience of isolation. Also, being surrounded by evidence of the instability beneath the surface (ash, larva fields, huge crevasses in rock) was both unsettling and fascinating. These threshold, emotive spaces informed my approach, however I can never be sure (nor can I obsess over) how much of this is translated into my images.

You have work coming up at the Melbourne Art Fair in August. Can you tell us how this came about, how you chose the work?

The work for MAF, '*P-O-R-T-A-L on my forearm*', is an extension of my last series, *subcompact*, which I finished in March this year. Both series include constructed material images located against those of actual bodies. The intention was to foreground relationships between force, density and pressure as I treat skin, muscle, bone, plaster, paint and clay all as materials to be reconfigured, smashed, erased and rebuilt.

The process of selecting the right set of images is actually more time consuming than taking photos. What I always do is shoot the same thing over and over with slightly different exposures and from very slightly different angles and distances. I then use Lightroom to rank images, different filing systems to collate my options and spend days moving images around on imaginary white walls in Photoshop. I find pairs of images that work together and I then build it up from there. Once the images are selected I then obsess over the particularities of the overall composition, including image sizes and gaps between images.

An important development for me is that the spaces between the images in 'P-O-R-T-A-L on my forearm' is wider than ever before and I've chosen not go with a double row hang. I'm thinking about relationships forming between the images, but hoping the images can also stand-alone. I want them to be assertive and singular in ways they might not have been before.

What else is planned for the next year or so?

I have a few smallish groups shows coming up later this year in Perth and one in Berlin. I have a solo show planned for the first half of next year with Turner Galleries and, hopefully, another in a Melbourne space. I've just begun making the work for these solo shows and I'm appreciating the long lead-time. I'm also looking into the possibility of making a small book and developing a series of images specifically for this format. And maybe a collaborative project with someone I really admire. And maybe even a music project (think Mogwai and Xiu Xiu, ha, maybe!). More importantly though, I am really concerned with exploring the interface of the personal and the impersonal in my work more and more and seeing what comes from that. That is what is driving me right now.

Jacqueline's work will be exhibited at the Melbourne Art Fair between the 13th and 17th of August, 2014. Her work can be previewed on her website (http://jacquelineball.com). For enquiries, please contact Turner Galleries, Perth (+61 8 9227 1077, http://www.turnergalleries.com.au).

Ahimsa Timoteo Bodhrán

Nueva York/Lenapehoking

Cañón

Sometimes she looks up through her tenement window at the projects across the way, their red brick against blue sky, and she thinks she is home. Mesas cut and beveled against turquoise. The street, a dry arroyo. Riverbed-quiet in the early morning. One day walking home, she swore she saw corn, over a story high. A girl could reach out her window and eat it. Caseríos, they call them. Shaped by man, true, but still, these stones, they never left her.

The Wall in Need of Protection

Beautiful, the brother, this evening.
Backdrop of brick.
What more need we to frame the living?

South Bronx Breathing Lessons

may I be a community garden
in my people's lungs
one two quick pumps on the respirator
swimming in the east river *before land fills*
oil covered *such clean children*
my family believing asthma's a myth
my mother hacking & coughing all her days

oh what vivid imaginations
so much more than penny candy &
pizza for a quarter
we had

north night sky

Grandfather, each night
you created;
to increasing light;
to anchor me here,

I look up at the work
arrows guiding my eye
I use it
this bedrock born
before these buildings.

history

The original purpose of the Bronx Zoo was to house animals.

Riverdale

How many of us
died here; how many still
in the service of whites?

Abuela

Hunts Point, Mott Haven,
and Soundview are not just the
homes of dead rappers.

perspective

telephone lines without sneakers on em
strange
you'd think they wuz made that way

possibility/maxim

If you can find beauty
in the way spit freezes,
you can survive
this city.

perspective 2

Mailboxes that ain't been punched in yet…
Buzzers that work…
No tape on the windows even…

    High class joint.

common (or myth of the calles)

Only diamonds
can cut
diamonds. your con-
crete shapes me from coal.

perspective 3

My spit on the sidewalk looks beautiful,
but pumpkin, sunflower seeds
on a bus floor will always
disgust me.

zipcode reality check

Despite rumours to
the contrary, Riverdale
is part of the Bronx.

why i wanted skywalker for a confirmation name

Kanien´keha heard high
  up in the skyscrapers
    language hovering above
      us
    ancestors drifting down
  abuelo en el cielo
shimmering night sky

human history II

Angels tell us: Ellis was not the only island.

'Ain't no In-di-
          -ans in NYC'
I go to speak
but only half
      m-
          -y mouth
              is there.

Robbie Coburn

To Madelaine

morning then
drive of dark rain   from the ceiling

      collects in waves on linoleum floors.

you look out

    into the repetitive   plot of the water

ripples breathe into one another

      scarce music of impersonal words

evaporate on a surface

    being lifted by the fumes

I lap with my hands,   looking out,   breaking

    water for those to come after you.

they come bearing   their tired deceit,

     the wind that lines the skull   and hollows

through with gullcries and harsh   distance.

a calming room of tidal regret,

we both   stop looking.

The Invisible Sister

1. Father, Daughter

Father, listen to the years
ploughing the grass at your feet encircling
creases in your skin melded by long winds,
a gathering of drought and memory that knots
in the horizon, a kink in the land you worked.
the sun slowly turned from brightness and charred
the foreground, shifting grasses beneath the sodium
glow of Summer.

the gallery of your raw mind
shapes the sinking backyard, the slow pulse in your
blood, your eyes reveal your brattled bones, unwillingly,
they soon gather back your dream of a severed motion
from your breath, the merciless past floods through
your interrupted veins, now simply an unnamed wound,
that hole that I fall through when it recurs.

my nameless half-sister, stripped of her body,
peeled from the animated glass: her
flesh and childhood belonged to you.
there was your leaving, the escape, then, underneath
a cacophony, reflected in the entrenched gaze of
your forlorn eyes and her drifting into an abandoned
search, your new life.
she must talk of your name, wound in her blood
and banished from your family. her father is a stranger
whose skeleton passes through memory, unrecognizable.
the onward devastation appearing, countless visits
and phone calls, a column of pillars you recognized

when visiting the court to resew the past. still
you went on.

the farmland stands, and yet the house is lit up
by low voices, space is established, stars themselves
fizzle out before your window, the remnants of blood
stains long buried layers of your skin. you lived in these
old rooms when I was only your future, stalks that fray
and starve in need of change, still, not a progression of a
forgetting. I miss what I have never known, and it lasts,
releasing the weight that doubles against your repaired
heart, you find her some forgotten night then wake
only to this.
the longing belongs in the forgathered illusions,
shadows I will watch sweep back into your suspended skin,
the distressed close up of a father's lips stitched into his
daughter's hair, which the eyes have sacrificed in order
to live. we all dance for less —
it's nothing you hadn't foreseen.

2. The Doubled Question

the night sky is a blank, unbrushed canvas, early,
but slowly, the stars unfurl, collectives
scattered around the obscured half moon pushed
through the cloudy hue.
it does not revolve, stitched into the gold-flecked sky,
revealing circled edges every hour or so.
the dimly lit screen shows land beyond the window.
an open door is swung into place by the filtering winds,
the air is cooling outside and the trees sway with throes
of sleep. laying here awake, life is unchanged
yet in the vast air out there this same question we ask:
where are you?

3. Sororem

I woke from months of searching
at a distance that is unimportant.
my still dreaming mind walked a flat
and uninhabited stretch of road
past the hollowed gum trees lining her
property. the strobed lights were
like welcoming voices. her own children
asleep inside the house. a pulse bursting
inside me some night when the urgent
moon eclipsed the stars. I reached her
at the bay window in the front room
and stared from a distance that
distorted the aging features.

4. The Invisible Sister

I never met your mother
we swept   light from eyes
each   year blurred faces
bridges lengthened water shallow
we grow aware of each other
your name is all I have of your
mother   and father   together
the revolving game called searching
she hates him more than you could
sister still   pray to meet   today
I love blood from   such distance

Helga Jermy

Sudden Shower Over Ulverstone Bridge

As I bend in those lines of sleet, hold the fragile skeleton
of shelter above my head, a twig snaps in etched
vertical slashes, fish fall in droplets, bounce
off the stillness of us into the river's mouth.
From my vantage, I am suspended
On the open bridge, agape in night air
lost in my colour, headed home before time freezes.
All the distant mountains stand weak and horizontal in nocturnal hue
a lone fisherman draws in his line, rows for safety, and we are
fully sketched, heads down, heads cold, heading off.

Susan Adams

Puppet on a Wire
Abu Ghraib Prison Torture 2004

I am like a gumnut doll
my head wears a cap
but it has an electrode
and my fairy dress is a cowl
It doesn't matter
whatever the garb
I tap dance on a soap box
until I fall off
and hang myself
on the wires
of another's arousal.

Mark Roberts

prehistory

i find the fragments and tag each one
the smallest are placed gently
into small zip locked plastic bags.
i lay out my bones on the sterile metal table
my legs down here my arms over there
my spine — just so

i take pictures, infrared and ultraviolet
carbon date the smallest sliver.
i am bleached and stained brown with age
i learn nothing.

Á. N. Dvořák

The Ruin

It climbs and reaches
This vine-like thing
That wraps itself without, from within.
Penetrating every soft and yielding flesh
So the crumbling halls become
More parasite than host.
It spreads, impends, advances,
Ensconces what was light,
And blackens deadened doors.
Curdled mists of lost, remembered
Hang in stagnant wafts
Of stench.
No foot longer falls on these rotted floors
The cobbled stones interred to earth,
And boards are clod, and moss.

A sudden pigeon's flurry,
As if spooked by the silence of it all.

This once-grand palace, this kingdom that was
Reclaimed by the slow decay of things that grow.
Is there any place more abandoned
Than one which was once adorned?
And grand, and bright, and loud
With flush-faced cheery drunken revel,
With flaming beds
and happy walls,
Not noticed for their soundness,
Now brittle, and cracked,
and no-one calls.

Andrew Bifield

The Car Will Not Start

The car will not start.
We can hear him
From the beer garden,
Trying to get the engine to turn over

Without flooding it.
'It's not going to start,' says Brit,
Looking at her empty cigarette packet.
'Why doesn't he just call a mechanic?'

She doesn't understand
Poetry.

August, 2013

Today is no day for metaphors;
My hangover so near
The wheel has sharp words with the kerb. The cops
Knock on your neighbours' four doors down.

Did I lock the car?
I think, and your calves lead upstairs
To view the baby's room. Your husband steams
Pork buns in the kitchen.

The exposed beams…
We haven't been in love
So long you didn't know I don't eat meat.
I pass on tea; the conversation,

kind, like strangers have
with one another. I miss being young enough to think
Anything will last forever.

Ashley Capes

Thunderclap

I do not have you
except in the half-dream
squeezed between a lunch break

and the next class
where you are asking me
to lift you up
onto my shoulders

who knows exactly
what colour your hair

or whether it would be winter
with frost lurking on bench seats

or whether I would
be gentle enough

and who knows
if I am writing this to naught
but a heroically white cloud
or whether you'd be
hiding in the coming spring

I cannot plan for your small steps

each a thunderclap
in my chest

Dean Meredith

How to Spot a Pervert

- We are masters and mistresses of disguise, and most adept at looking normal.
- We have excellent eyesight, might still wear glasses, and may or may not have mentally undressed you, while looking you straight in the eyes and without you knowing.
- We are highly fashion conscious, and dress so badly we neither make statements nor try to be ahead of our time.
- We are experts in the bedroom; however this only applies to the subtle moving and positioning of furniture.
- We are great lovers of food and can cook, eat and drink, all in the one kitchen; but we are not gastronomes - that would be showing off.
- We prefer our own cars to buses and trains. In our own cars we can pick our noses in private.
- We know about art, including films, music and painting, but we don't always get it.
- We are inherently lazy creatures, and prefer watching TV and sleeping to anything else.
- We like libraries, because the books are usually quiet.
- We detest public toilets - they are impossible to find and inevitably by the time we get there, we have a new traumatic experience to share with our psychologists.
- We have families and friends who we don't really know and who don't really know us, and that's probably just as well.
- We are incredibly shallow people with deep thoughts, strong hearts and weak minds.
- We are natural cowards who go places we shouldn't and feel more than we should.
- We are not nice, but those closest to us think we are. Fools – at least we share that in common.
- We aim to be strange, but not different, and often just settle for weird.
- We are everybody and we are nobody, except for those times when we're somebody in between.
- We are actually impossible to find, unless you're one of us too.

Ashleigh Synnott

Plumb Thumb

                        Pick someone
               and put him under a tree.
    Keep him there for a day;   take off his pants
                    make him stay
    make him do the very thing he don't know how
                    and give him
             something for his troubles.
             There are plums up there.
                 (Say this to him.)
           Fruit you can reach, purple.
             And then give him one.
                 He can't reach.
His legs are too tiny; no hairy to hasten the wind up his backside to force him
                  to move away
               from the ground
             the dirt is just fine.
                   Is it fine?
               (Ask this of him.)
   Wait to watch him sink baby teeth in ripe flesh
     coloured fruit and then say, of the plum:
            Is it pretty inside you?
          And watch what his eyes do.
              Do they follow you?
             You should be afraid.
                  Little boys,
              under plum trees,
               without hands
            and without height,
        should stay on the ground.

Christopher Konrad

Rene T and Dog Investigations

And all this endless labour — to what end? To none save to bury oneself ever deeper in silence, so deep that no one will ever be able to drag one out of it again.

As I read and tried to digest this typical Kafkaesque ponderance, I couldn't help thinking of Rene T. I also thought, staying with K, who's to say where the investigations of a dog will lead.

Deep. Talk about deep 'n dark, like that movie *Pitch Black*. Did Rene T get to that place that K was talking about, where ten stallions couldn't pull her out anymore? I don't know. I hadn't heard either about her or from her for over ten years.

I often considered that Rene T's self-destitution, her exile, as a kind of Great Wall of China: endless, stretching as far as the naked human sight could determine and perhaps even further, far as a migratory bird could fly and that her self-mollification would not only be as long as that damn wall, but as high *and* as heavily guarded.

Eleven years ago. We were dating. I use the term in its loosest sense in that we met each other almost frequently enough to make others conjecture that we were, in fact, an item. She had just emerged, as if from a long, long night of illness, from a quagmire of excruciating relationships. Everything, or so I thought, was a long summer evening. Three years of yes, and a picnic hamper of till-the-last-star-goes-out. She was my first and, so she said, I was her last. We played the 'what-if' game all the time.

'Rene T — what if I found someone else…'

'Well Mr K I'd have to forgive you wouldn't I; I'd want to know is she a red-head or a brunette. I guess I'd have to check in and see if you would be up for a threesome…'

'Don't joke about this shit Rene.'

In those days we couldn't rattle each other. For some reason we were impervious to the possibilities of what any day could serve up. We weren't serious. We were too serious: everything was life and death; nothing mattered. We lived, as they say, off the smell of an oily rag.

Rene T's relationship-before-me number one — Paul. Control artist by profession and by personality and, looking back now from the clear hindsight of distance, perhaps this relationship laid the foundations for Rene T's Great Wall, and provided its mortar. Indeed, if foundation-of-suffering be the metaphor for Paul it makes it even sadder to know that he was her first lover, the one who should have flung the doors to life open; break down walls (not construct them) and allow his girlfriend to scream in ecstasy after the years of barred adolescence and pre-pubescent purgatory. A freeing from the commandment *Thou shalt not* and not the installation of further parent-like Mosaic stone-legislation. But this was not the case with Paul, whose incessant barrage of questions was matched only by Rene T's capacity to burrow ever deeper into the volcanic soil of her immolation, like the blind mole: *where did you go today? who did you go with? why them/him/her? how much did you spend? What? That much, and then you complain you need the money*! Every new question becomes like a blow to the head and him getting all delirious and punch drunk (although, he never laid a hand on her - he didn't have to, of course). Sex becomes hard labour, a curse even — and K's words erupt in my reminiscing mind… *And all this endless labour? To what end?*

One day, after a seemingly endless forest of one-days, a year later, looking like a decimated or deciduous Chinese Tallow in mid winter, one of Rene T's friends dragged her up and out of what passed for a relationship where Rene T was furiously laying the foundations for her future Great Wall — the Great Wall of Rene.

Her next attempt at life, her second in the great chain of non-being: Charles. What can I say about poor Charles and then immediately, and with no less sympathy or horror, what of poor Rene T? If Paul helped lay the foundations and supplied the mortar, Charles supplied the stone work. Massive boulders of recalcitrance, reluctance and self-recrimination. Quarries and quarries, truckload after truckload of self-loathing, endless self-pity and unrequited self-hatred. O yes, Rene T had gained her freedom all right: no longer wired round and barbed by vicious mendacity of the razor-darts of suspicion, envy, vitriol. Now arrived the chisels and crowbars of denial and self-imprisonment. Not of Rene T, but of Charles by Charles.

Now the questions came from Rene. 'Why don't you get out for god's sake, Charles?'

'And do what Rene? Do you have any idea what I'm going through?! No! So shut the fuck up!'

'Charles, you're so talented. People would kill to write and play music like you do.'

'Yeh, right. Do they want what comes with it Rene? Are they prepared to pay the price?'

Charles did not savour the broken artist card as much as he enjoyed fishing. In fact, he was more of a fisherman than musician. He would cast his self-derision into a very wide and open, waiting sea, like so much burley more often than not reaping only driftwood or tangled seaweed, but, fairly frequently, he would pull his favourite catch: the prized Great Rare Rene T.

The stone wall, now waist high and stretching only from the Jiayuguan Pass to the Zhenbeitai Tower. However, soon, it would be complete

Time is immortal but self-derision is a patient and inexorable sun beating over us all, until some cataclysm comes and splits a canyon into a range of broken rock. In the case of this story, the cataclysm came in the form of a truck driving into the side of Charles' car as he cruised along the Brookton Highway. Ironically, this event did not deter Rene T's wall-building, but seemed to enhance and hone her masonry skills even more.

Soon, whole valleys of her landscape were over shadowed by her wall-building because sunshine could no longer reach certain parts of her country-self. Trees were stunted and a steel-cold wind blew where once gentle breezes swirled and delightful pools were filled with colourful fish surrounded by frondy ferns and green-white eucalypts. So long ago: how old were you then Rene T?

As I watched the progress of Rene T's marvellous work which finally erupted with catastrophic results, I asked myself, as K had many years ago: *How long will you be able to bear the fact that the dog race keeps silent and always will keep silent, as your researches make you increasingly aware*? Indeed, my own dog investigations have uncovered the fact that, as with K, the sole response we can ever really expect from those around us is a harrowed silence. That was certainly more than I could offer Rene T.

I got up, went to work in a kind of 9 to 5 stupor for months, years. Not being stated anywhere along that lengthy time was the fact that I was falling: a quiet, desperate death like Thoreau's men or the waning Willy Loman. I knew it, my boss knew it, the whole damn world knew it, as even Rene T did and maybe I had become just one last loser to cross off her list. I tried. Well, I thought I tried; not to be Paul, Charles or number three, Drew, but who knew if I wouldn't be the four thousand guards buried with the Emperor? As I think back now though, the wall, after Drew, was well and truly up and the Empire well and truly secured.

Loser four hundred and fifty four: out the door.

Somewhere along the line the play between us took on a decidedly new tinge. When it was time to get serious I must have been standing in the wrong line. I was shooting for eighteen or so; unfortunately she was heading towards thirty.

As much as I tried, with the limited stock of emotions in my repertoire,

Rene T was the expert in that field. I think she could have written that book: antagonistic, annoyed, angry, guilty, disgusted, anxious… guilty. Wow. That last one came up a lot. It took me ages to get her to shift on from that one and slowly, I mean minute by excruciating minute slowly, she eventually forgot even how to spell the word. But I clowned and clowned my way into another form of anaesthetised state. While her guilt was learned behaviour my particular penchant for acting the funny guy was an addiction. Rene would call it a compensating mechanism. Her therapist taught her that little gem.

'You know Chris, Melita reckons you use your clown act as a screen.'
'I thought she said I was compensating for something.'
'No *I* said that! What are you hiding?'
'You know all sorts of dark secrets…'
'And there it is.' And with that Rene T left the building.

On one hand I was kind of proud of her. For standing up to the shit factor, getting out. On the other hand I felt like the loser I somehow knew I always was.

'One day Chris, when you've decided to grow up and be a man, let me know. Maybe then we can have a conversation, let alone a relationship.'
'O yeh, and you'd know what that is, Rene!'

Sticks and stones might break bones but well constructed and aimed sentences with just a touch of sardonicism (read: arsenic) could well and truly maim and, sometimes, kill.

&

As I said, it has been ten years since I last saw or heard from Rene T, but last month I received a letter…

'Dear Chris, sorry I haven't been in touch…'

What do I care, I've moved on, haven't I? Rene who? Wow.

K says: *we survive all questions, even our own, bulwarks of silence that we are… with my questions I now harry myself alone…*

Yes. Living alone completely has its advantages. It means not needing any consolation or having to give it; not thinking of the other person day, noon and night. Not thinking of walls or trench warfare, minor skirmishes or cataclysmic battles.

Rene T and I, after her catastrophe-boyfriend number three Drew, had what I thought was a beautiful thing. We moved in with each other very soon after we met at the Seventh Street Cafe. She was a friend of a friend. She was down and out after a string of what could only be referred to as toxic, if not lethal, relationships and I, I was coming to the end of a six year cycle of trying various ways of fitting into a world that didn't seem to either need or want me. Ways including:

1. Working and studying myself into oblivion
2. Several disastrous one-nighters
3. Drinking and smoking myself into another oblivion
4. Avoiding relationships — *all* relationships
5. Living in a coastal town in a rundown boat shed

They say love is possible. With the Book of Rene T I became a believer. It seemed easy: weekends at the markets, French movies, trips south along the coast and winters in little beach houses belonging to family or friends. The whole cliché.

Her letter goes on about depression. It went on at length about Paul, Charles and Drew and… the burning sensation of love in a real relationship (yes Chris that would be you). Words began to fly over that Great Wall of China like so many paper aeroplanes. First of all, just some words, but then squadrons of letters with both of us, in turns, flying lead.

The wall she had built seemed all but impregnable but bit by bit a gaping hole wore through it with the barrage of paper.

'… I think I'm ready for what we had — if you think you can do this too…'

How did she know I didn't already have a fantastic relationship?

That I wasn't married with four great kids and a fantastic wife?

How did she know I wasn't already on the road to a mellow and settled old age with the love of my life?

Then the clincher letter. Like a Book of Revelation.

'Chris, I know I'm responsible for the wall you have built around yourself, that awful silence. I don't blame you for not answering my letters after we broke up. I was wrong to leave you. I was wrong to hurt you…'

Wall? What wall was *she* talking about? That massive thing you could see from the moon stretching like a mountain chain across China that she had so completely and unilaterally constructed out of death, vitriol, bitterness and abscess? Who was she kidding? Wall *I'd* built. Wow, talk about denial.

I sought answers amongst my friends; the one or two who stuck it out with me over the long winter after she'd left. Ray, friend number one.

'What is she talking about, Ray? Who is she kidding?'

'Chris, get a grip man. Don't you remember when you smashed into that tree after you got her message that she was leaving? You cut out every single friend you ever had. The only reason Dan and I are still left standing is because we promised each other not to see you kill yourself!'

I waited a few days and went back to my faithful investigator dog K; *but what good are all these questions anyhow, for I have failed with them completely; probably my comrades are wiser than me, and employ excellent means of a quite different sort to endure this life… but where are these comrades of mine… where are they? Everywhere and nowhere. Perhaps my next door neighbour…*

It took me a while to get it straight, to get it in my head just how long I had been in the wall-building business; to remember just how many letters Rene T had actually written and how many I had failed to answer. Let's try one hundred per cent.

As I went over this letter again and again just to make sure I was getting it right. To check my bearings and to quadruple-check I was ready to get my guts ripped out again. Was I grown up enough for Rene T? Was she hoping I was?

We have a date (I use the term in its strictest sense) to see each other next week. At some cafe I've never heard of before. I'm not sure where this will all head. I'm not sure how much grinding wear and destruction those ten years have already extracted but maybe that's for some future investigations. Other Ks and other dog investigators.

Ian C. Smith

Alison Long Ago

During the manhunt for bushranger Ned Kelly
your father as a boy attended police horses
in the stables and paddock of his father
the doctor who had a piano hauled
over crude roads to echoes of curses
up those hills a heaven of eucalypts.

You received a marriage proposal from a chief
tactfully declined on a South Pacific isle
saw the goodness of the world stripped bare
as an almoner between the wars
hair grey ecstasy of brief marital unction
before finding him felled with no goodbye.

Up early visiting us you startled me
without your hair a convincing wig
wanted me to write his biography
but I was Ill-equipped though flattered
aware of bookmarked texts you read
in sheltered accommodation
rising young talent like Peter Carey.

Your handwriting crept into a swirling future
the same news repeated exactly.

Memory-tossed I think of your life loved
two in the morning wrapped in the black night.

Jan Napier

Reframing Frida

This marriage is limned in salsa de chipotle.
Less abstraction
less internalising would help
you go about your own affairs
as el elephante does his.
And perhaps la paloma
you know heat often numbs pain.
First up Friducha some electrolysis please.
Now off with thorn necklets
smack monkeys   backhand them away
smooth Panzon from your brow
pluck out his arrows
redness clots soon enough
even though some wounds stay open.
Brush away blue tears   paint in champagne
orange blossom   earrings from Picasso.
Unmake your bed   be comfortable
the damaged don't need hospital corners.
Coronets of roses   costumes of papaya
and banana style you Aztec and royal.
An end to dolor   let down your hair
laugh out loud.

Stu Hatton

vectors

        Water on
        stone,
              water
        in stone.

              *

        Vapour-ascension,
              cloudscape &
            rain.

              *

        Curvatures of leaf,
              petal
        form the watercourse.

              *

        Seed-time:
              seeds rain wider,
        wider.

              *

        Forest of messengers.

*

    Traffickings &
        filterings
    of light; webbings
        of waveforms.

*

No one moment
    or movement
  prevails.

*

Canopy over ferns
          over soil:
    shadow
upon shadow.

Jim Davis

Future Lemons

The bowl of eureka lemons was meant to be
        painted. I stroke a towering cumulonimbus, wispy
stratocumulus creeping beside as the sun
        sets gray & blue — on my way to date #2

with the same girl, paint on my hands, engrossed
        in rush-hour swarming like slow roaches — dividing
distance traveled, in feet, by the current state of Middle-
        East relations, translated from Spanish, then USD.

The radio says *Bendecire, Andalucía*, one of many women
        I'll soon forget. I tap the dash when the Spaniard says
he prefers his fathers fried, fathers with cheese, his belly full
        of fathers. The center lane holds, stoic in its unchoosing.

Fucking traffic & a fathom down's a death measure —
        6 dark feet, can you imagine? Once explicative sail-claps
say little, ring against the semi-truck with chrome curled
        exhaust pipes like two smoking horns. I U-turn & park.

She's been waiting for me. I tell her boys like to explore.
        Two bottles deep we wind our hands together like ivy
over keys on a ring, considering a cheese plate. *What's this
        one for?* Together we bite her nails, other things

connect — what's riveting's riveted to the flag pole, mast
        tacit, sinks — *Go like this*, she said, hiding an ice cube
in her napkin, massaging nonsense from purple lips & teeth.
        I regret what I will pluck from her & ring like future lemons.

Jeffrey Alfier

Farm Girl Harvesting Ryegrass at Sixmilecross

The sky harbors rain somewhere east.
Hers for the afternoon are pastures

pressing horizons to their raw limits,
fields of light cut with May winds

and sparrowhawks that hunt the hedgerows.
The sun breaks through a shoal

of belated storms. She pauses, tilts her face
toward the warmth, turns back to windrows

rising in soft hummocks left for the combine's
gathering. In the late cooling hour, she will close

the jacket at her throat, make her way
to the forage wagon that fronts the fields,

convey the harvest to silage; her hands,
lean as harrows, locked in the slipping daylight.

Karla Linn Merrifield

Aubade in Nine Amphibrachs

I ponder dawn, listening, repeating
his koans in amphibrach whispers:

> *I'm writing*
> *the troubles* —
>
> *Your brother*
> may be *your killer* —
>
> *into the music*
> *into the music.*

In *December*'s
blue raincoat he arrives.

> If *my woman*
> *is sleeping* and dreaming,
>
> she is *much older*
> and *nobody's fool.*

Humming Aurora's love song
with the poet, the old monk *remember*s to chant:

> *I miss you,*
> *forgive you* your enrapture

glad you *took the trouble*
to say your morning prayers in my name.

Sincerely,
L. Cohen

With lines from Leonard Cohen's 'Famous Blue Raincoat'.

Sue Clennell

The Maidens of Artemis

She said it was against her will
but Callisto has been fishing for the stars
casting her line loose and expectant
cooking with gaffes   flirting with flesh
and now she is round with child.
Ha! She thought she was pepper perfect,
Artemis is not pleased.
Ho Callisto, you will be cast out
and you will find there is no peace
in quiet.
Artemis will put the heavies on you.
You thought you would kill snakes
and climb ladders.
Begone with your bold, boxy ways.
The child and you are winless,
your tears are too late.
Smell the remorse.

Mike Greenacre

Preston Point

I start my journey as a poem
suddenly thrown onto the page
on a track by the Left Bank Hotel
East Fremantle foreshore,

the sky as my opponent
threatening rain as I climb up
the cut limestone steps
behind the brawl of voices

as if I'm entering a hidden
land   shielded in part
by it's proximity to now:
Tuart, Peppermint, Fremantle

Mallee, Rottnest Island Pine,
Sheoak and other inhabitants
have adapted to life here
drinking discreetly between

high alkaline rock and sand.
Walking east along the limestone
ridge formed by nature's
sculpturing   from compaction

and leaching of marine deposits
beneath the dunes that have
disappeared with time's
accomplices of wind and rain

the Swan River's meanderings
have carved out a rock-face
that stares back with
beauty's rage.

A waterfall coaxes my
steps, through green and
variegated leaves, down
a series of levels it plays

then gushes forth to the
river shore at Preston Point:
'Niergarup' — Noongar for
'the place where pelicans meet' —

a 'Bush Supermarket' before
the arrival of the white spirits
who fenced off their land,
restricting their blood-flow

as land grants swooped as crows
down to the Canning or Swan
River shores claiming sacred
sites and traditional hunting grounds

'Noongar territory' and people
with different cultures and
beliefs now herded as cattle,
suddenly thrown into one.

And do we feel Yagan's pain
when trust and friendship
were betrayed? It was here
at Preston Point that he

vowed revenge for his brother's
death   Yagan's head was to
carry a price tag of 30 pounds —
'for a working man, a year's wage'.

MIKE GREENACRE

I started my poem as a journey
thrown onto a dirt track
beneath the dunes   that
ended at a ferry crossing.

Allan Padgett

I Dream of Jeannie

It was a three-way tussle
        on the lounge room floor
        a triangle, massaging feet and calves
and then, thighs,
and then, ...
        bits of Buddy Holly
        further bites of 'when I was sweet, ...
            sixteen' ......

Fingers gripping on the muscle
        fickle boundaries fading fast
        passion stepping up past reason
        you'd think it were the rutting season

He moves over, probes and kisses
        sets off a niagra falls of lust
        limbs engage, lips fuse, fire sparkles

Me? I'll just observe, thanks for asking
        my role in love as in life
        is to become the facilitator
        the encourager
        the interpreter — my hand holds the pen which
            scribes the play
        your hand holds the joy you are seeking
        your fingers probe the swamp you need

Massage her into you
        divest your shoes
        make lust your companion

Seek hot depths together, be as one
    I am inside yet outside, it is lovely
    I am robust, I am brave
    fuck her hard, fuck her deep
    many long years have passed since your first hunger
    now it is time, well past time, to be sated
    nay, to be mated

Probe long my anxiety
    thrust deep my fears
    kiss my flapping ears
    tickle my hairy balls
    finger my desperate arse
    suck my rock-hard cock
    hold my:

        attention

Have fun
    dare I mention

        She is mine.

Stephen Pollock

Weltschmerz

He was known as Mr Sudsy — the washing powder tsar of Yorkshire. People in the North East were in awe of him, they regarded him as the Donald Trump of detergent. The nexus of his empire was Hull, Grimsby and Scunthorpe. Mr Sudsy called it his soapy Bermuda Triangle. It's rumoured that his personal fortune was in excess of £25 million.

Harold turned the page and continued to devour the fat police dossier.

Mr Sudsy likes to dress up as Vera Lynn and eat bridies while prostitutes watch him masturbate. He claims to have slept with over 300 women. He is a sex addict, or as our generation like to call it, 'a mad shagger'. Phil Minker, Soap Suds regional manager.

The intercom on Harold's desk began to blink.

'Harold, Mrs Marigold is on the phone, she's asking if she can make an emergency appointment with you this morning?'

Harold sighed. 'I had three sessions with her last week, what's wrong with her now?'

'She says the voices have come back and the begonia on her windowsill looks like Frank Bruno.'

Harold groaned. 'Book her in.'

Harold assumed his favourite seat on the 5.15pm express train to Hull. He opened his leather attaché case — the same one he had carted around for 25 years — and placed the Sudsy case file on his lap. Where was he? Ah, yes, page five. Mr Sudsy had just abandoned his third wife and registered yet another business — 'Fishy Fries. Yorkshire's premier cod-flavoured snack.' The fiasco was short-lived: Smiths, who owned *Scampi Fries*, initiated legal action and forced Fishy Fries into a bumbling retreat. Mr Sudsy retaliated by launching a range of Yorkshire-inspired sodas. The line included Red Bollocks and Miner's Yank, an energy drink containing burdock, mustard and Guarana.

Harold's chuckle attracted a glance from the seat opposite. He was normally tangled in *The Times* crossword by this point, somewhere between five across and an aneurysm, with a look of glazed resignation. The passenger tried to glimpse the case file, but Harold sensed the man's incursion and shifted his knee, shielding the file with his grey flannel suit.

He scurried to the appendix, eager to find out what Mr Sudsy looked like. He was somewhat disappointed to find that Mr Sudsy was actually quite handsome, but not in the conventional sense: he had dense, curly brown hair, ruddy cheeks and a ten-bob smile. The clothes were Yorkshire Hollywood: chequered sports jacket, Paisley-pattern tie and a pair of tan bellbottoms. Harold's career had taught him that most lotharios were not overly attractive; they relied on psychological and vocal artillery. At the age of 14 Harold had discovered, to his eternal disappointment, that girls went for silverback gorillas, not pseudo-intellectuals. The man opposite peeked over his spread-eagled newspaper. Harold elevated his leg, bringing into view an old school photo of Mr Sudsy. He immediately recognised the sallow paint on the gymnasium wall. It couldn't be… Sat on the front bench, with his hands clasped on top of his scuffed knees, was a timid Harold, wedged between the future mayor of Grimsby and a local dermatologist. Grinning on the back row was a young Mr Sudsy, surrounded by the class wags and his girlfriend Jenny (the only girl in primary seven to have nurtured two hummocks under her school jumper).

A violent jolt shoogled the train carriage and sprayed the contents of the case file onto the floor. The passenger opposite slipped off his seat and crouched on one knee.

'Allow me to help,' said the nosy stranger.

'It's okay,' blurted Harold, his grey face now flushed with emotion. 'I can get them.'

In the subsequent fumble, the school photo shot under the seat and disappeared beneath a carriage heater. The stranger continued to fuss.

'You know, we sit in the same carriage every day but we never talk. I'm Nigel. I work for Barnaby and Joyce Accountants in Grimsby.'

'Harold, I work across the road at Sinker Psychiatry.'

Harold reluctantly shook the man's hand, then scowled at the photo of Mr Sudsy trapped under his left Hush Puppy.

The bus that shuttled between Hull train station and Harold's middle-class tomb took around 40 minutes. He sat on the top deck, peering out at the muddy flats that flanked the River Ouse. He wondered if the boy in the school photograph was actually Mr Sudsy—the dolt who had teased him incessantly at school? Such parallels were easily drawn by a 48-year-old man, who, by virtue of age, would often find himself dissecting the past, rather than embracing the future. Harold drew a squeaky circle on the misted bus window. He peeked through the hole and saw his younger self playing tennis—strong, emerald eyes; palomino thighs and a pinch of steel…

Harold was brooding in his study with a large Glenlivet. His wife was next door, enjoying an episode of *Lewis*. The file peeped out of his attaché case, but Harold was determined to ignore it, and pretended to leaf through a periodical instead. Reading about Mr Sudsy's life reduced his to a dreary whimper. The phone on Harold's bureau began to jangle. It was his 'hot line' that clients rang in the event of an implosion; but recently Mrs Marigold had been pestering him with tales of a satanic gerbil.

'Mrs Marigold, how can I help?'

'Is that Harold Sinker?' said a male voice.

'Yes, whom am I speaking with?'

'I am an old friend of Mr Sudsy, I just wondered how you were getting on with his evaluation?'

Harold lent forward and rested his whisky on the desk's leather carapace.

'Sorry, I'm not at liberty to discuss that, patient-client confidentiality and the court case is pending, would you li…'

The calm voice interjected, 'I'm sure you'll do a great job. In fact I think you'll find that Mr Sudsy has a mental condition that will absolve him of all responsibility.'

Harold's single malt began to lap against the walls of his crystal glass.

'Do you think your shitty little practice got this case by accident?' continued the voice, this time with a slightly gruffer edge. 'Mr Sudsy made sure that his evaluation came to you — his wimpy ex-classmate. You are going to help us out, Harold. You know it and so do I. You were always the last pick at football — things haven't changed.'

'Wait a min…'

The phone line went dead. Harold sat in silence for several seconds before gulping down his nightcap. He reached across and plucked the case file from the attaché case.

Maybe the call was a hoax: one of his old classmates who had seen the court listing in the *Grimsby Herald*. He galloped through the case file, until he reached a gory anecdote on page 52.

Although Mr Sudsy is predominantly a charmer and womaniser — he had kissed the Blarney Stone in his pampers — he has a predisposition for violence which can flare up at a moment's notice. During a Soap Suds sales conference in Cleethorpes, he bludgeoned an employee with a three-litre carton of detergent after catching him texting during a presentation. He went berserk and used any implement within reach as a cudgel — repeatedly whacking the man with a toilet brush, mop and sanitary towels. I will never forget that pink effervescence, as the blood mixed with soap powder on the boardroom floor. That day, he made Caligula look like Bill Oddie. Tony Furk, Soap Suds managing director.

A brief pillage of the case file revealed more violence and skirmishes. There were also dalliances with the Yorkshire underworld and a slew of unpaid alimonies. It seemed that the glare of the police had been on Mr Sudsy for some time, but his heavyweight political connections had always kept them at bay. Mr Sudsy wasn't just a rich farceur; he was a rich, violent farceur. There was always a hint of a fly undone, but now he was wielding a tyre iron in his right hand. Harold yanked open the bureau drawer and grasped his vial of valium.

&

Over the next fortnight Harold began to reread *Lolita*. During a torpid Sunday lunch with his wife (the kids had promised to come, but cancelled at the eleventh hour again) he had begun to ponder Vladimir Nabokov's inspiration for the novel. He had been moved by a newspaper article — probably in some émigré broadsheet — that told of an ape that had been raised in captivity and taught to communicate and perform human tasks. When the ape was given a sheet of paper and a set of crayons, it sketched the bars on its cage. On hearing Nabokov describe the incident, Harold felt such empathy with the primate that he nearly burst into tears. However, his pity was tempered by his own reticence, and he only managed a dignified sniffle.

'Harold, would you like some more gravy?' enquired his wife from the stern of the dining table.

Harold gaped at the faded certificates and photos that peppered the walls. Now that his two daughters had left home, all that remained was the detritus of what had always been a flimsy marriage.

'Harold! Would you like some gravy?'

'No, I'm fine,' he muttered, ushering some peas around his plate.

The ape lingered in Harold's brain; it wouldn't relent. He pictured himself drawing on a sheet of manila — he had sketched his iron bed frame, with a set of L-plates on the headboard.

'Good, Mr Ape Man,' said the white-coated operative. 'Now put the banana in the slot.'

Harold wrested the keys from the zookeeper and bounded out the door.

'Harold, where are you going?' yelled his wife.

'The study! I need to phone Mr Sudsy.'

The night before the trial arrived with the air of a doctor's waiting room. Harold was lying in bed with the case file strewn over his ill-fitting pyjamas. His right eyebrow twitched at will and two generous sweat patches adorned his oxters. He washed down a handful of diazepams with some tepid hot chocolate. The tension of the preceding weeks had induced vomiting, weight loss and chronic masturbation. He extended each of his fingers in sequence, trying in vain to tot up how many opiates he had taken that day. Finally, he regained some sangfroid, and peered down at the case file. A final skim would ensure there were no holes in his testimony. Despite the imminent risk of death or imprisonment, in some perverse way, he was actually starting to relish *The Adventures of Mr Sudsy*. It had all the reckless drama of the Old Testament. He thumbed to the lewd, page 72.

Sudsy would regularly hold orgies in his Alcázar in Scunthorpe. Everybody would attend: the local police commissioner, mayor, minor politicians, Russ Abbot—all of society's casualties. One party he waltzed in naked, wearing just cricket pads and brandishing a King Eddie cigar. He got everyone to slather themselves in bay oil and play Twister in the buff. No expense was spared and he hired Black Lace to play in the conservatory. I can distantly remember Mr Sudsy getting a reach around from a Maggie Philbin lookalike. Tom Tunt, Mr Sudsy's chauffeur.

Harold looked over at his pallid wife: the tight perm that vibrated with every passing snore, the washed-out nightie that hung off her shoulders like a Marks & Spencer's pall. In his twenties he had a wild fling with a Jamaican hussy at Hull University. He had wanted to marry her, but society and his parents disapproved. Instead he had settled for a Caucasian wallflower. He glared down at his wife's thin lips. He wondered if he should leave her behind tomorrow? Harold sighed, rolled onto his side, and quietly masturbated. He eventually reached a meek climax somewhere off the Caribbean coast.

&

The gentle shunt of the train lulled Harold into a state of childish bliss. Outside, the green countryside flashed by unannounced. Suddenly, his mobile phone began to vibrate. Harold tried to ignore it, but he wondered if it was the police — maybe they had caught up with him? He swiped the phone from the seat, squinted at the text message, and sighed. He started to tap a reply, but the words wouldn't flow. Since he had turned 45 the latency between his thoughts and fumbling prose had steadily grown. Eventually he ditched the fancy Latin and went for the jugular.

'Mrs Marigold, Harry Secombe died some time ago. In any case, he did not wear leather chaps and certainly did not waggle a purple dildo. Please take two valium and go straight to bed. I am going on a long holiday, please contact Dr Tartae in my absence.'

The carriage door clattered open. Harold flinched. It was the train conductor: a tall man with a fat, inviting face. Harold fished the tickets out of his suit trousers and surrendered them with a nervous smile. The man inspected the tickets and quickly handed them back.

'Merci, Monsieur Sudsy.'

Harold chuckled as the man retreated into the passageway. He sank into his seat and closed his eyes. He was glad his little ruse had worked: his false testimony had persuaded the jury to acquit Mr Sudsy on the grounds of mental illness — Harold fondled the leather briefcase on his lap. It was crammed with the money he had extorted from Mr Sudsy to lie in court. Later that day, his anonymous phone call to the police revealed that Mr Sudsy was an old classmate of his, making his testimony void and triggering a retrial. By this juncture he was already 500 miles south of Hull.

For the first time in years Harold felt a gentle throb in his undercarriage, a nubile flutter in his chest — the first pang of adolescence.

The carriage door clattered open again. Harold spun round. It was his wife, clutching an Eccles cake and a plastic cup of tea. She zigzagged across the carriage before lurching onto the seat beside him.

'I thought the Eurostar was meant to be smooth?' she protested.

She perched the cake on top of her Dick Francis novel, then slurped her milky tea.

'Does it rain much in Antibes? I forgot to pack my light jacket,' she inquired, nibbling the perimeter of her cake.

'No, Vera, I don't think it rains much at all. I think the weather is going to be just fine.'

Aaron Furnell

Home Truths

Sat on an arse caning wooden bench seat
in an Elephant's Garden
not so distant from that far flung Terrace in the North
across that infamous road, in fact
from that infamous place where cunts go to live and die,
     infamously as they please
I chuck a dart in my mouth
and watch two beautiful lovebirds carrying on in courtship
dancing that dastardly dance of DTF.
I realise, not so suddenly
(For this epiphany has long haunted my thoughts)
as I am sat with a dirty durry on my lips, unlit
and a pint of dirty Irish ale, near skint
that I have never been a lovebird.

For how can a scumrat transform, just so?

Ivan de Monbrison

Untitled

équivoque mirage cette stupeur qui t'accable
  ne te ressemble pas
mais raconte un autre désir
d'être absent de soi-même
  défiguré et pur
l'angoisse qui s'oxyde au contact du temps
le rêve qui émerveille le fou
  qui soliloque
et dit
la beauté ineffable d'un monde distribué
aux paresseux passants qui se laissent griser
   mais ne s'abandonnent pas à lui

equivocal mirage this stupor that is overwhelming you
  doesn't look like you
but tells another desire
 to be absent from oneself
   disfigured and pure
the anguish that oxidizes in the contact of time
the dream that amazes the soliloquizing
 fool
who says
the ineffable beauty of a distributed world
to the lazy passers-by who get exhilarated
    but who don't indulge in it

« The Night »

Écran liquide d'une pensée, lassé de la refléter, le corps cousu à sa blessure, laisse sortir la cicatrice, est-ce une bouche ou un sexe? Le saignement du monde coupé en morceaux comme une poire laisse s'échapper des pépins. Le corps se creuse de sa douleur, la nuit bascule à l'intérieur de l'orifice abandonné. Une marche qui emmène la route, me dépose au pied du vide, là où les ombres dos à dos observent le monde circulaire. Les gants qui attachent mes mains à l'objet qu'elles manipulent donnent à manger aux silhouettes dégarnies d'hommes édentés par la souffrance. Un enfant couvert de cendre circule entre les cratères laissés au sol par ma folie, ses yeux ébahis observent l'univers peints sur ses paupières, il ignore que derrière celles-ci se dressent la nuit infinie peuplée d'épaves de chair et d'oiseaux aux ailes de sang.

Liquid screen of a thought, tired of reflecting it, body sewn to its injury lets come out the scar, is it a mouth or a sex? Bleeding of the world cut into pieces like a pear lets go away its own the seeds. The body is dug with pain, night switches inside the abandoned hole. A step that takes the road away, deposits me at the foot of the void, where shadows back-to-back observe the circular world. Gloves which tie my hands to the object that they handle give to eat the bald silhouettes of men made edentulous by suffering. A child covered with ash circulates between the craters left on the ground by my madness, his amazed eyes observe the universe painted on his eyelids, he does not know that behind them stands the infinite night full of wrecks of flesh and blood-winged birds.

Vanessa Page

Maranoa

i
Morven blood moon
he stares down
at a plate of something fried

ii
Outside Mungallala
two young boys
sever a wallaby's tail

iii
High noon
the sun strikes the river
like rifle fire

Colin Dodds

Not Just Stars

The week started in a cosmic motel,
but the cosmos isn't just stars
It's big rocks crushing smaller rocks,
sleazy deals between the jackrabbits and the sagebrush,
clouds gathering like a lynch mob

The ghosts of unmourned dinosaurs rise up
deformed and deranged in the Joshua Tree boulders

The cosmic rental car and the cosmic waterbottle thud
along the concrete panel freeway, vibrate like a dying virus

The sunset lights the layers of sedimentary rock
to spell out the unwelcome notion
that this story isn't necessarily about us

In the heat, the road ahead is a plume of steam

Kenneth Hudson

My Front Verandah

Opening my morning front door I find
overnight   my verandah
    has become a purple pool
       of Jacaranda flowers.
Rippling waters of lilac perfume.

Inside
my cracked leather mud-caked boots
clomp across the wooden floor.

I leave by the back door.

Ben Walter

The Rock

face so cracked
bones
land} settling
puttied fractures shantied
vegetation
flat shaved stones
obese wind
g} with us
our air
lunged water
fraternity}

square body
blown dirt {land not
(captured) in wounds
(captured)
verdant deceiving
gulls cycle (captured)
at {G
sinking
kelp (captured)
enforced {paternity/
outcrop locked.

Roger Vickery

Family Court Orders

dress him in a lead lined suit

shower him with fresh mown quarter acre grass

polish him with a number two cutter
that hates dead paint

fill his holster with family snaps

stop him calling

wild cat falling

nails screeching
on suburban glass

suddenly unreal

as anti-matter

Carl Palmer

Senior Moment

I just had a senior moment.
I didn't forget something,
I remembered something.
I just remembered how my mom
would see or hear something
reminding her of something I did
when I was small, get that smile
in her eyes, look back and
picture me in my cowboy hat.
"Stick'em up, Mommy."
I remember her senior moment,
as she explained it,
not forgetting, but remembering.

Now I have them, a visit back,
a reminder, like it was yesterday.
My senior moment begins
as I watch the young mother as she
herds her 6 children, 3 boys and 3 girls
across the street to the old brick church,
checks each one before entering,
stops short, kneels down
in front of the oldest boy,
turns his head side to side,
holds his chin, takes a tissue
from her purse, licks it and
rubs the smudge from my cheek.

Libbie Chellew

Early Signs

Arthur brings the shovel down on the neck of it. The fact that the boy is behind him doesn't cross his mind. It isn't until the rusted bottom edge is forced through the flesh of it that Arthur hears a whimper.

He has no tolerance for wimps. The boy's natural reaction to witnessing the death of something for the first time goes ignored. The boy, Rory, would be silent next time, or possibly the one wielding the shovel. Sometimes to be violent is to be humane. No better place to learn that fact than with Grandpa.

'This is the best way,' Arthur says and looks up.

The boy's shoulders are up.

'If it's going to die anyway,' Arthur says, 'you'd just be weak to sit by and wait.'

The last time Arthur had done this, it was a joey. But you don't see them in Greensborough anymore. That might mean the boy doesn't need to see this at all. Arthur can imagine that argument coming from Nicole, Rory's mother. But she'd be ignoring the overall problem. There's little meaningful death here because there's little meaningful life.

The boy is staring at the body of it, waiting for him do something. Arthur has a splinter in his palm from the shovel handle. He rolls the skin of his left palm with his right thumb and forefinger. It's set in deep and he feels it in his flesh as he rolls pressure on it from either side. Arthur considers what to do with the carcass. The sun rages behind him, the heat on his neck makes him think of cooked flesh.

'Find me a decent stick, will you?' Arthur says over his shoulder as he wiggles the shovel underneath the limp head of the thing.

Rory appears next to him and hands the stick over without looking up. He is hopping from one foot to the other, still looking at it. The bitumen is hot on his soft young feet; Arthur can feel the heat through his slippers. Rory springs back over to the nature strip.

The stick is weak and too short but Arthur manages to use it and push the thing onto the shovel. The lower half of it, the flat half, comes off the bitumen easier the he expects. He uses the stick to curl the thing's tail back over itself. Arthur can feel a pinch in his lower back as he pulls up from leaning over. He stops for a moment still leaning slightly, and then starts to walk towards the bins. The carcass balances on the end of the shovel. Arthur breathes through his nose in short whistles. Rory keeps his distance, running down the brick path to the front porch. Arthur opens the green wheelie bin and lets the carcass drop inside. There's blood on the shovel and blood on his left slipper.

'I'm just going to hose this off,' Arthur raises the shovel at Rory. 'Off you go.'

Arthur goes to the tap at the side of the house and leans against the weatherboard as he bends down. The tap shudders and then sprays water in all directions. It's cool in the shade and he can feel particles of water land on the top of his foot and his ankle. The splatter makes a pattern on his slipper. He puts the shovel under the tap, watches the blood drip, diluted, and absorb into the soil. He twists the tap off, which seems to take more twists than it did to turn on, and leans the shovel against the house. He hesitates, scratches his nose crease and then walks back to the front. He slides his slippers off at the door and walks into the house, the carpet surprisingly warm beneath his feet.

Rory has put on one of the DVDs he brought with him. Arthur doesn't bother asking what it's called; it's animated. He doesn't sit on the settee either, making his way through the family room and into the kitchen. When Arthur shuffles in front of the screen and Rory ignores him. Arthur's moving a little slower, not used to being out in the heat or using the old heavy shovel. He's paying for it, with each step his lower back twangs and releases heat.

Arthur makes a thick lather with the soap at the kitchen sink, letting the water run while he does it. He takes the hand towel and dries his hands before cleaning up the small mess he created making their vegemite sandwiches for lunch. The sides of the margarine container give easily as he grasps it. It shouldn't have been left out. He shoves the breadboard under the tap to rinse and then takes the soft pink sponge and wipes down the bench in vigorous strokes. Rinsing the sponge he watches the white breadcrumbs fall to the plughole, absorb water, and wash away.

He decides to wipe down the sink and the taps too. Then he wipes down the microwave and the stovetop. He takes his Thursday apple out and rinses the Kiwi Fruit hair from the fruit bowl. He rinses the sponge again, watching as the dirt disappears, and the sponge reinflates, looking new again. He takes the sponge and pushes it into the groove between the bottom of the windowsill and the tiles and pushes it along. He runs the water again and is satisfied to see a grey mark resisting the rinse. He places the sponge on the edge of the sink and then runs his damp hand through the thinning hair on his crown.

Arthur takes the cola Sunny Boy he bought for Rory out of the freezer. He had to negotiate the dollar out of his budget by buying one apple instead of two for the week. He snips the top off and takes it into the family room. Rory is asleep, his brow concentrated and his arm hanging off the side of the couch. Arthur sighs and takes the Sunny Boy back to the freezer, leaning it upright on the interior shelf. He shuts the freezer door carefully and makes his way back into the family room. Rory doesn't stir as Arthur turns the volume down on the television so the movie is quiet.

He sits on his armchair next to the couch and lets Rory sleep. The television screen reflects the front yard. Arthur thinks about closing the vertical blinds behind him but the cord is stubborn and would make the kind of noise that would wake Rory. The colours of the movie are bright and soon Arthur can't see the front yard in the screen anymore. He sees the landscapes made of lollies and two characters, a muscled man who sighs with his whole body and a small black-haired girl with big eyes. They're sitting on the branches of a candy cane tree discussing something in earnest.

He recalls his wife's love for hard-boiled sweets. He can see her at the lolly shop in Warrandyte, or Sassafras, buying jars of yellow pill-shaped sweets and red glass lollipops. He thinks of the tin she used to keep in the car. He can hear the crunch. He watches the muscled man snap and break the delicate sweets as he walks through the lolly world. Arthur wonders what Rory will learn from films like this. Arthur thinks about his wife and her mad driving. He thinks about her.

When the credits start and the screen goes black, Arthur looks over at Rory and sees he's still asleep. Rory's lip quivers. Then his whole body shudders and it makes Arthur lean on the arm of his chair and stand up. As he watches, Rory's mouth lets out a low moan. Arthur can hear Rory's tongue inside of his mouth, clicking rhythmically between moans. He doesn't believe waking Rory up is the right thing to do, even as the moans become more urgent. Arthur stands over him and watches. Rory moans, letting out some deep distress.

Through the window Arthur sees his daughter Nicole's Dualis turn into the driveway. He looks back down at Rory, who's still moaning, and feels he's going to be implicated in this. He sighs and walks away, opening the front door quietly and meeting Nicole on the porch.

'How'd you go today?' Nicole asks, smiling. She shakes her hair off her face, puts both hands on her hips. Arthur can see the stubble under his daughter's arm and the half-moon sweat mark on her red linen top.

'He's asleep,' Arthur says and nods toward the window. They both look through and down on Rory. He looks still for a moment and then Arthur sees his lip quiver. He looks up at Nicole but she doesn't react.

'We're going to have to go straight away, though,' she says and knocks on the window. Arthur watches the boy. Nicole knocks again and then bangs. Rory jolts and sits up.

'Yoohoo,' Nicole says so he turns toward the window. He looks from his mother to Arthur, his expression blank. Nicole turns to Arthur.

'Are you well, Dad? How are you doing?'

'I'm just fine, Nicole,' he says.

'I'm wrecked. We had some winners through the ER today. We had a guy come in through triage claiming not to have slept in three days. He reminded me of you.'

Arthur breathes out his nose and nods.

'Three days, though. I nearly didn't believe it. No drugs. Just can't sleep. His wife was hysterical about it. The couple ended up screaming at each other. Dr Pratt said he saw a patient with similar symptoms earlier in the week. Isn't that strange? Two in one week.'

Arthur looks at the wheelie bin, in full sun now, and wonders about the stench. He hears Rory come out the wire door behind him.

'Thanks for having me, Grandad,' Rory says and nudges Arthur's elbow with his shoulder. Nicole smiles at them through a yawn. Arthur nods at Rory and meets his eye for a moment.

'Come on,' Nicole says. 'Thanks again, Dad.'

Rory follows his mother to the car. As he passes the wheelie bin, he turns his head and shoots Arthur a look. Rory makes a silly face—showing his bottom teeth and looking to the side—as if the carcass was a joke between them. As if he'd just said, 'whoops.'

Christopher Konrad

Seidel Doesn't Care (ad honorem)

Seidel doesn't care   dives in to say what we don't dare
Do I ?   at least (I guess)   I am unaware
Of his panache an' all
And *dare me do*   maybe he's old and not long to go
But I am young with a lot to lose
(do I   am I   old /young   who knows)
But it's good to have a larff: for instance, he says
Let me masturbate to death/ let my hand fall off
Haha   what kid (or guy or gal)
Can't relate to that   but what is this pomp and do
Pompidou: when in France do as the French do
And so   all my life is a circle (or square or trapezium or something)
And so   to care and not to care
This is the question that Comrade Seidel throws – like C4
In my general direction   he's all wired up
Ready to greet his particular red-head or seventy virgins
(about which he writes a lot: either that or Japanese schoolgirls
don't anybody ever say Seidel is nothing if not multicultural)
And so   do I care when one of his poetry-bombs goes off?
Do I do medoobeedeedo

Richard King Perkins III

Diary of a Sensitive Youth

In Cody
I remember the woman with no teeth who was crying.
I wanted to give her a couple of cigarettes
or maybe even the whole pack
but then I wouldn't have any, so I kept them,
and I moved on.

In Spokane
I was living at the park with the other homeless people.
Me and my friend were showing off
to the college girls that passed by
but I got tired of that
so I climbed a cliff about thirty feet high
and when I stood on top I could see the whole city
and when I looked down I saw a kid about my age
wearing black Converse shoes
his body covered by a ripped orange tarp.
His hands were on his stomach, cradling his severed head
and I said, well, at least you can't feel anything—
but I wasn't sure who I was talking to.
I couldn't speak for a couple of days after that
and one night, by the fire,
I noticed that I was wearing black Converse shoes,
wrapped in an orange poncho
and I knew that I would never talk again
if I stayed there, so I got up,
and I moved on.

Outside Spokane
I gave a woman my last five dollars because she looked like
the woman in Cody who I wanted to give cigarettes to.
But even after she had the money,
people still turned their heads from her in shame
and I thought, what difference does this really make?
Five dollars might last half-a-day
and then she'll still be the same anyway.
I was totally broke now, and I wished
I hadn't given away all my money, so I made a note,
and I moved on.

In Denver
I was sleeping at a friend's place
when I heard gunfire and jumped up and remembered
oh yeah, this is Denver, and went back to sleep
not too bothered by the drive-by-shooting.
In the morning
I heard that a little boy had been shot in the crossfire.
I was sad in a way
and wanted to do something to help.
Three weeks later, I was still there,
unable to think of any way to help, but I heard
he had gotten better anyhow and I felt better,
so I lit-up a found, half-cigarette, inhaled,
and began moving on.

Ross Jackson

Castrado

At two ounces, had it gone for his hand
the strength of its
neglected dog's bite
would not have been great
and had he ever worn
that black beret
he'd paid for thirty years ago
in Barcelona
its awkward presence at home
would not have shown
as shame in his face

and had he ever had the cojones
to display it in public
it would not lie on a shelf
like a burnt pancake
becoming a cursed fetish
cutting him with this refrain:

the rock stars of the 60's are still rocking
or are famously dead
but you are not bold
or spontaneous its presence says
you are not Latino, or sensual
not bohemian, or creative

you fear loss of pride in being noticed
and in the blazing corrida
of each morning
as you look into your wardrobe
you are humiliated
by that empty scrotum
of black felt.

Raven Current

In Someone Else's Words

1. 'Time Becomes Meaningless Without a Sun'
When I set out on this trip, I planned to come back. I remember the high, the vertigo. The first warning: *Do not eat the food,* which I did, of course.

I picked up my bag and boots after running. I tripped on the lip of plastic. A uniformed young woman caught me, gripped longer than was strictly necessary, and played a familiar tune: *I love you, I love you, I really do.*

I fell asleep. I dreamed the room was flooding. The floor became an ocean, cold.

I woke cold, unable to see, hear, or sense anything, not even my own weight.

I observed the crowd, like so many dogs. One trotted over, licking and wagging behind me. He circled several times, chaotically. Catching my eye, he glanced down. The gap between us would only grow. Now suddenly we were apart. A chorus of one.

I was dizzy nervousness, a version of myself, a yo-yo-like sphere.

It was not the first time in my life that I was invisible. As a child I learned to blend in, perform, on desperate day. With my first pang of worry, I felt as if I could stay a thousand years or twenty minutes and it would make no difference. I had never felt so disoriented: no sun, no East, volcanic tongues of red, gray, black, and white, like old friends. I had yet to learn the laws of recognition. Apparently the dead were incapable of paying attention to anything for very long.

I fell asleep. I dreamed: galaxies.

When I awoke I was sore from sleeping. It seems life can change you so much you wouldn't know yourself.

In eating the food I had inadvertently closed off.

2. 'Surroundings Can Change'
In the endless day and night I have forgotten something among the dead. How can I continue this way without knowing?

In order to know this world you must be able to play.

3. 'What We Cannot Speak'
Life quickened in common indecipherability — between event and memory, between all sides of the story, the living and the dead, childhood and everything else. The subject of silence formed an unacknowledged nucleus.

I imagine a mountain can look different in the light, as so many villains and clowns.

4. 'It Isn't What You Think'
Waiting for a message long enough to remember: what's done is done.

I saw it all again, vividly, a welter of images like overlapping nightmares. The persistence of the present.

Moving and yet static, I find myself here. I simply fall and that is the only way of knowing the moment of death, like an exhale.

I remember the chaotic vertigo, the drama of consciousness. Who, what was I mourning? 'I' became a fiction.

There was a knock on the door.

5. 'Blowing Bubbles'
Love.

6. 'The Middle of Nowhere'
There is no middle of nowhere. The human compass, searching, in vain, at last became aware.

7. 'Blind Spots'
I have taken off and am walking free – no longer in search of my ghost.

Human.

Still.

A cento sourced from The Spokes *by Miranda Mellis.*

Bruce McRae

Forgotten Promise

After the rainbow,
a pillow stuffed with dreams and mites.
A carnation dipped in gun oil.
A request from Death's neighbour.

After the rainbow, a meteor.
Scuffling among the cutlery.
A village swallowed by the countryside.
Spectres sparring.

The rainbow, painted on a cellar wall
by the blind sorcerer's daughter.
Under a tin bucket of milk.
Remote and indifferent
to men's strife and the causes of suffering.

After the storm, a rainbow.
Walking a tightrope. Twisting a wire.
Mocking the sounds we make
before nightly retiring.
As peculiar as lost money.
Like finding a finger in the snow.

The one that shows itself at night.
The deer's god and raven's deformity.
What the prisoner on the gallows saw
through the folds of his departure.

Cameron Lowe

The Lillies
For Jill Jones

Strange lilies   on a polished table   leaning or bowing
real and imagined   as if a breeze had touched

or woken   the creamy-white of living flowers
red-streaked   at their edges   too heavy

for slender stems   in the glass vase   a face
I once knew well   as clean water turns

the grey-green of twilight   sky curving
inward   and over   the shapes

of the lilies   the old vase
wild with the plunge   of dark birds

A New Room for Spring

even with your teeth
in the cup

on the lunch tray
you are not yet

a thing for science —
September again

you mumble
'I've just lived

too long
for this world…'

but the body
goes on

and we watch
Nureyev

and Fonteyn
spin by

purple flowers
we can't name

swaying beyond
the glass —

Phillip Ellis

For Stuart Barnes

Music as oily as frying bacon
drifts from the passing cars into night air,
then it dissipates like the smell of food
just upon the tipping point of congealed.

In the inner west's suburbs, it's winter.
Sydney is less cold than it is wary,
its lights treat the horizon like a fence
that perves on the rentboys that flinch from hoons.

One day, our friend shall wake with pain curdling
in painful kidneys, and he's pissing blood;
that's the price for voting for such men
who hire faggot-bashers as the police.

Mather Schneider

Almost Everything

I have wine, pozole and clean air.

I have a beautiful woman with eyes as bright
as a toucan's laugh
skin as gold and moist
as tequila on the bicuspid
of dawn.

I have 9,000 personalities
and the hundreds of eggs they lay every day.

I have truth like the thumb
of all things.

I have half
of two bodies
on a hot mattress
with clean blue sheets.

I have siesta dreams
that make me sad
the afternoon can't last forever.

I have ancient blood around me
that shines like new.

I have this long hot desert
the cactus that rise so slowly
like they couldn't care less about love
or like.

I have my lies
that mesmerize me in my weakness
and my efforts that thicken
my watery soul.

I have moments of strength that come upon me
like a sudden storm
I have people that care
even if their care doesn't understand
I have people that will walk through fire for me
even if that fire is of their own making.

I have almost everything
most of it is unutterable
silent and dumb.

It is so much that if I give it away
it becomes more
and if I hoard it
I become a hollow place
without even an echo.

Danielle Spinks

The Benley Acquisition

I'm at the bar, chugging orange juice with my mates, and we're laughing at each other's pov jokes. *Nuns Frightened by Change*. That's the name of Friday night's band at the Landula Criterion. Our band, as it happens. It's our first gig. *The Nuns* are two mates in my year and me. I'm called the percussionist. That means I play drums and, occasionally, I whack a thong on a bongo.

Next week we start work experience. That means no school for two weeks. I was one of the lucky ones who found a placement. Gareth had to go to the meat packers and so did Kev. So it's kind of a celebration gig. For me, anyway. Without the alcohol.

We're up next, straight after Gordon Finney. He's the Mayor. He's having an Extraordinary General Meeting.

The mike squeals. 'Hiya!' Donny says. He is our resident monobrow.

'Top to see ya all. Tonight's gunna be a great night. We've got *The Nuns Frightened By Change*, a local act, all Landula boys, born and bred, barely outta their nappies…' He looks over at Gareth who likes to wear his jeans low. I don't get why he likes to flash the top of his Y fronts. He's a mate, but he ain't no Justin Bieber or anything.

'No, maybe not quite out of the nappies…' Blah blah blah. Donny's a dickhead.

Here comes Mr Finney. He looks like he wears women's foundation of the orange kind — the stuff seen on *Days of Our Lives*.

'Ladies and gentlemen of Landula.' He's got a new microphone ring. A great big chunky one that flashes out to the crowd. It flashes into my eye. Geez, Finney. Ya bling could blind a man.

'I told the wife this evening to shut the bloody door. "Why?" she says. "Coz I caught five flies in here already this evening. Three of them were male and two were female," I say. "How the bloody hell d'ya know that?" she says. I say, "Coz three of them were on the beer and two of them were on the phone."'

I've heard him tell that one three times now. And I don't even make it a habit of listening to his speeches. If anything I try to avoid them. But they're unavoidable. He pops up everywhere. Someone opens a cake shop — there's Finney to cut the ribbon. A new house gets started, there he is with his gleaming shovel. The town donates ten bucks to the midgets of Miffaworfoo, there he'll be with the big fake cheque.

A few guffaws from the audience, and an especially loud one from Shirley Mason. Fiona Cassidy is up the back. She looks like she's smelled something foul. She's wearing a hot pink business suit with black edges around the lapels. *The Nuns* have our own secret awards. We call them 'The Landies'. Even though she's really pretty, Fiona wins the Landie for 'Filthiest Fashion Sense'. Finney ties with Farmer Kelly for 'Ugliest Man'. Shirley Mason? If you saw her you wouldn't be asking. 'Most inaccurate lipstick applier? Most gargantuan blonde in the over 50s category? She's be a contender for both.'

'Ladies and gentlemen, now Let's Get Serious!' Finney thrusts out two open hands either side of the mike. Open hands. Sign of sincerity.

'Landula is facing a crisis. This year, Landula Primary School has held a fete, half a dozen chook raffles, a cake stall, and a dance contest.'

There's a round of applause. So many fond memories, I guess.

'But why, people? *Why?*' Finney's an ace public speaker. He lets the tension build up when no one answers. It's an awesome technique. Makes tingles go over you. It's like advertising. It's all Sell Sell Sell.

'What? For the tuck shop? For gucci new sports equipment? Well, where are they? Bring it on!'

People are ordering beers but other than that, it's quiet. 'I'll tell you why then. I'll tell you why they're expending so much energy and time on these kinds of events. I'll tell you why, people. They're having to fundraise for their most basic expenses: Chalk. Paper. Wages.'

He'll just let that land for a minute.

'Landula Public Library. Same situation. It's bought no new books for nearly eight months. No new books! What's a library without books! The only new books have come from personal donations and bequests, and if it keeps going like this and any more Fletcher sisters fall off the perch it'll be all Mills'n Boon and no natural history.'

A greater silence. Until Shirley Mason knocks over a beer at her table.

'Why? Because the State Government doesn't care about little places like Landula. It'd rather see us disappear.'

'Benley Shire's got it worse than us,' Roger McElroy calls out from the bar. Ever seen Star Wars? Remember Jabba the Hut? I'll say no more.

'They do. But you know what they've done about it? They're expanding their copper mine.'

'Well good luck to 'em!' Roger says into his beer. 'Yeah.' Finney takes off his spectacles and looks at them as if he's deciding whether he wants them or not.

'Yeah, good luck to 'em.' They're brown transition lenses. With the spotlight on him, they're practically sunglasses. He starts wiping them on his tie.

'Do you know what will happen a year or two from now? When Benley is pulsing with change and new growth and Landula continues to slowly starve on its paltry funding?'

He puts his glasses back on, hands on hips. 'It's goodnight Alice! Landula will be subsumed by Benley.'

It takes a few moments for this to sink in, because the beers are doing that. Then people charge to their feet and beers are knocked over left, right and centre. There's disbelief. Shock. Indignation. That's because Landula people hate Benley people. It's nothing personal. No one throws eggs or anything. It's just a Shire thing. And as far as we know, Benley people feel the same way. So the idea of having Landula become a part of Benley is pretty bad to us.

'So here's what we're gonna do.' Finney interrupts the racket, both hands jutting out as if he's measuring the one that got away. 'We're gonna do our own acquisition. We're gonna make a PR pitch so effective that even Benley people will vote for it. Benley Shire will become Landula Shire. And I've hired our very own, very impressive Entice Events to do it for us.'

Fiona Cassidy stands up and starts applauding. Oh God. Suddenly my glass feels very heavy.

That's the firm I'm doing work experience with.

Monday 8.50am
Fiona is at work first. Then me.

Mum made me arrive at 8.45, not 9.00, in order to make a positive impression.

It's a two-room office with mushroom pink walls. It's a bit on the crappy side.

'It's a dump, isn't it.' Fiona is jiggling a tea bag for me in the little kitchenette. I'm close enough to pash her. My face is red and, because my hair is on the reddish side, it isn't a good look.

'No. Not really.'

'Used to be a massage parlour.'

'Did it?' She steps on the bin's foot pedal and dumps the sodden tea bag in, then hands me a mug which reads *Entice Events* and with a drawing of a swoosh and a shooting star on it.

'Thanks.' I take the mug.

'Did you work here then?' She lifts a nostril at me, an open gesture of hostility. Why did I say that?

My cheeks are burning so I go to the dunny to check them in the little mirror. I'm a beacon.

9.20am
German Karl arrives. Then Boyd, the league player. He's the manager. He's wearing a nice suit, but with basketball shoes. No jacket. Mental note – trainers are okay.

10.00am
We have a meeting at the wooden conference table. We all bring our teas. Fiona brings the bikkies.

'How are we gonna convince Benley people that they want to be Landula people?' Boyd.

'We've got to make them want to.' Karl.

'Oh, DER!' Fiona opens her notebook.

'Let's make a mind map of options. We'll have a brainstorm.' In the centre of the page she writes 'Landula Job'. Boyd leans over and draws a circle around it.

'Okay, brainstorm,' he says. 'The floor is open. Pump 'em out.'

I feel like I'm the new boy on the stock exchange floor and I'm supposed to jump up and down yelling out prices. But I'm embarrassed. And I don't know what any of the prices are.

'Make Benley jealous of Landula,' I submit.

'Tarnish the town's reputation so that they'd rather not be associated with Benley anymore.' Boyd.

'I'm not puttin' that down.'

'It's a brainstorm. You're supposed to put everything down!'

Fiona, in capital letters, writes 'EMBARRASS – THE SHIT – OUT OF BENLEY'.

Boyd leans over and draws a star around it.

Fiona's fringe is shaped like a flower.

'What else?' she looks at me. Her skin is tanned from years of holidaying in Bali and Surfer's Paradise. 'One suggestion isn't a brainstorm.'

Her suit today is yellow and covered in large magnolias.

'Haven't heard from you yet, Karl.' Boyd picks up an iced vo-vo.

'Make them fear not merging with us,' I put in. 'We'll become a big town and they'll be the little backwater.'

Boyd clicks his fingers at me. 'Good one, Jase. Write that down, Fi.'

'I'm writin' it…except that, really, they'll become the big town and we'll become the backwash.'

'Stuff 'em. They don't know that.' Boyd, licking the pink crap off his bikkie.

'Everyone knows that.' Fiona throws a bit of paper at him. 'Stop that. It's disgusting.'

Boyd reclines all the way back in his chair. 'Let's just have a public boxing match between the two mayors. Gordon Finney versus Gerald Whittaker. Winner gets both shires.'

'May I ask, why do we need to join the shires anyway?' asks Karl. 'Coz if we don't one of us is going under. Weren't you at the meeting, Karl?'

Karl shakes his head. 'I don't like rock music.'

'We could dig up some dirt on Whittaker and get him to convince his people. Maybe he's a homo or something.' Boyd. I think he's serious.

'Wait a second,' Fiona drops her pen. 'Before we go any further, we need some research. Otherwise we're just gonna go round in circles. We need to know who our target is, how they think and what it'll take to make 'em vote for it.'

'Well Benley Shire is our target, ya fool.'

'Well when we find the rest out, that'll determine our approach.'

Boyd crosses his feet on the table. 'That's a good point, Fi.' He sucks on his pencil. Not just the end of it. A good inch or so.

'We should get a person from Benley on board. Someone who knows them, trusts them.' Karl.

'Like who?'

'Monica Metherin. The Natural Therapist.' It's Gordon Finney, standing in the doorway, a half-eaten hamburger in his hands.

'Monica'd be perfect. She knows the place, she's lived there all her life, and she's short of cash.'

'Great idea, Mr Finney.' Boyd jumps to his feet, shakes Finney's hand and starts circling the table.

'How about a television ad?' Finney throws in.

'Do we have the budget for that?' Karl.

Finney looks like he's about to toss us his hamburger to us like he's feeding pigeons. 'Sure.'

'We've never had the budget for a television ad before.' Karl again.

'If Mr Finney wants a television ad we'll give 'im a good quality one,' Fiona.

'I don't want to tell you guys how to suck eggs, it's your show. But if ya ask me I reckon Monica is just the ticket.'

1.20pm

Fiona phones Monica, gets her in and we start discussing the script.

'People need a spiritual underpinning for their decisions. They have to agree with the acquisition.'

It's not what Fiona wants to hear.

Monica quickly proves to be another pain in the arse. And she's a large woman. Very large. Elephantine, really. She's the Shirley Mason of Benley but with redder, straighter hair and without the beer burps.

'Jase!'

'Yeah?'

'Whadda you think?'

'I think…' I think her knockers must reach her knees when they're not all bunched up like that. Loose pandas.

'I think we need to just find one thing that's good about it. Then talk about that. So… I think the acquisition is the right thing because we can share resources and it'll be, you know, less stressful.'

'Good point, Jason, I'd like to flag that,' Monica. 'Benley people, like Landula people, want simplicity and grace back in their lives. The merging of the two shires will be a mechanism, a catalyst, for that return to spirit.'

'God, Ms Metherin, we're not killing anyone.' Boyd.

'Exterminate Benley. There's another option.' Karl.

'Would you guys shut up!' Fiona unscrews the lid of her water bottle.

'How do we link acquiring the shire with, you know, being spiritual?'

'Well, it's like a brotherhood, isn't it, darling?' Monica's words are like warm caramel off a spoon. They're long and syrupy and they land on you.

'For so long there has been this sibling rivalry. Now it's become unhealthy. It's time to put our pitchforks down and come together — arm in arm.'

'That'll look good,' chortles Boyd. 'Imagine Farmer Kelly and Big Ross.' 'Errr.' Even Monica can't help but quiver. She's grossed out to the max. It makes me laugh. She recovers herself.

'But symbolically, darling. Symbolically.'

'Maybe we need a bush dance.' Time for me to make another suggestion. 'You know, we give away a few lucky door prizes, get everyone dancin' with each other, everyone gets pissed.'

'Not bad, mate. Not bad.' Boyd. But he's not into it.

'I could get *The Nuns* to play.' Struggling now. *The Nuns* doing 'Strip The Willow'. That'll be the day.

'If you need a fiddler, Mary Allan is wonderful. Wonderful.' Monica.

Mary Allan is a 55-year-old depressive.

'Oh. No thanks.'

'A bush dance, yeah. Not a bad idea.' Fiona likes it!

'We'll have to write a speech for Gordie.'

4.10pm

Meeting's over. Finally.

Monica makes the 'closing ceremony' remarks. 'I think we've come together beautifully today and now we will simply massage the differences.'

The calendar falls off the wall.

Wednesday 5.30pm
We're filming the ad. Monica's doing the voice-over, on location, at Farmer Kelly's.

'For a hundred years, Benley and Landula Shires have co-existed, side by side, through drought, flood and war.'

Long shot. Late afternoon. Two farmers are hoeing in their neighbouring paddocks.

A chalk line on the tarmac between them symbolises their separation.

'And not always without some sibling rivalry.'

Farmer Benley throws something at Farmer Landula. Landula picks it up. It's a dirty apple core. Focus pull to Farmer Benley pretending not to notice.

'But now, the state coffers have tightened the purse strings and there's no relief in sight. And it's likely that one, or both of our shires, will disappear. Our small, close-knit community will be split, with many of our members travelling to the city for work that leaves us unsatisfied and homesick.'

The music, an austere banjo, crescendos, and a drum-kit kicks in, played by none other than yours truly.

'So, now more than ever before, it's time to extend the hand of friendship and unity.'

Long shot. Farmer Landula throws something at Benley who catches it. It's a shiny green apple. Benley lifts it in acknowledgment of his neighbour, smiles and takes a bite.

They drop their hoes and each walk to the road between them. The divisive chalk mark is inadvertently scuffed by their boots, and begins to disappear.

Monica steps into the medium long shot. She's wearing beads and an orange and purple caftan thing, like Mama Cass.

'Let's save our precious shires, our lifestyle, our community. Join with us by voting for Gordon Finney's "Union of Neighbours"'.

Camera pulls back. Sun melts into the horizon.

The waning sun shoots a star-shaped flash from the corner paddock. Beauty. End of ad.

The bit about the new shire being called Landula Shire and the fact that Landula was acquiring Benley to keep itself afloat, not to save both of them, well, we all agreed that was better in the 'round file'.

THE BENLEY ACQUISITION

Friday 4.20pm
'I'm lovin' it. I'm lovin' it!' Finney's pours himself a whiskey in the dark.

The curtains are closed. We've wheeled the telly into the office for the sneak preview screening.

Tuesday 9.16am
I'm at Landula Railway Station.

We have a big mediation meeting in Sydney. Evidently, I'm two hours early for my Sydney train. Stupid Landula phone service. They've given me the Saturday timetable.

Tuesday 3pm
At another big conference table, but this office is swish. I mean, fully swish.

Gerald Whittaker, Mayor of Benley, is here. He isn't happy about out proposal. Or the ad, which aired over the weekend.

'Now hold on Gerry. You're getting ahead of yourself!' Finney — always the height of diplomacy.

'You haven't even secured my consent yet alone that of the State Government or the Electoral Commission. What on earth are you trying to achieve?'

'Now settle down Gerry.'

'I beg your pardon!'

'Just take a breath. Look, I understand there's nothing in concrete. We are just keeping on top of things, okay. We simply want to send out a *feeler*, if you will, gauge the vibe of the kind folks of Benley.'

'Are you suggesting that television ad is a piece of legitimate market research?'

Finney looks like he has tasted something sour while he thinks it over.

'It's a bloody propaganda piece!' Whittaker snaps. He pushes his swivel chair back from the table.

'I'll be obtaining advice on this matter, Mr Finney. But I'd imagine you're too intelligent to do the same.'

Fiona makes an 'oooh' face as Mr Whittaker storms out.

Boyd slaps a hand down on the glass table.

'Well.'

'Well indeed,' says Finney.

He turns to us with disgust. 'See the shoes that guy was wearing? Got to be worth two hundred quid. Now who's ripping off the people of Benley? Is it really us or him?'

'Mr Finney, when Mr Whittaker said you were too intelligent to get advice, I

115

think he was doing some reverse psychology.'

'You don't say.'

'So that's why we're here.' She looks around at all of us. 'We are here for you.'

No one is saying anything. I look back at Fiona. 'Do we have a legal advisor?'

'He's our legal advice man,' says Boyd and slaps Karl on the back.

That doesn't quite make sense to me so I look back at Karl. 'I thought you left Landula High in Year 10.'

Karl is a beacon but Fiona snaps, 'Karl is very knowledgeable about the law. Aren't ya, Karl.'

Karl's all hunched forward. He only lifts his eyes.

'Yes.'

'Well,' with my point won, I raise a single eyebrow. I've been practising in the bathroom mirror and have pretty much nailed it. 'Aren't *we* lucky.'

Tuesday 4.15pm

Despite Karl's fantastic legal background and obvious skill and knowledge, Finney makes the surprising decision to see a solicitor.

'You can organise an election to 'merge' the shires if your constituents so choose, but you cannot 'take over' a shire. Benley is not a 'fish-and-chip shop', if you will,' says the suit. His jowels are bobbing over his too-tight white tie. He does the finger thing for inverted commas, which I personally hate.

'I'm not suggesting Benley's a bloody fish-and-chip shop.'

'Analogously, you are.'

'No I'm not.'

'I'm sorry, sir. It's unworkable.'

'How bloody ridiculous. It's a vote, not a massive drama. Unity of Neighbours. Shirley's designing the voting form right now. It'll be letterbox dropped tomorrow.'

'I don't think I'd recommend proceeding.'

'Oh, well. That's your opinion, isn't it.'

'Yes, sir. Yes it is.' Mr Finney stands up and walks over to the window.

We can all feel he's out of his league. Legal advice. Electoral commission. Geez. It's more complicated than any of us thought. He stares ahead, back to all of us.

'What's the objective of what you're trying to achieve?' ask the suit. He pulls his jacket sleeves and discreetly checks the time, but I catch him.

'Things are going under, mate. Things are going under.'

'The hospital had additional funding this year, did it not? The school. It had a new teacher. The government noted it in its rural and regional economic impact report. It was a case study, was it not? Things are going relatively *well*, aren't they?'

'No. No they're not.' Finney sounds like a broken man. Or a broken record. Not going well. Not going well.

'Well what's not going well? Essential services are in the clear, are they not?'

'Oh, bloody essential—' Finney waves a hand behind him as if swatting some imaginary fly pestering his back.

'Well what's not going well?' Finney's staring intently at the grassy area below. A dog squats down and a turd arcs out of its behind.

'It's the bowlo.'

'It's the what?'

'It's the bowlo. The bowlo's not doing well.'

'The bowlo's not going well.'

'It's not just any Bowlo.' He's annoyed. 'It's the centerpiece of our community. It's the linchpin. It's the whole town. It's the meeting place, the *espirit de corps*. It's everything to Landula. Everything.'

'Right.'

Mr Finney turns back to us. 'That Bowlo goes under, we go under.'

'I see.' The solicitor shuffles papers and closes a manila folder.

He clasps his hands together. Nobody moves so he stands up and puts the file in the filing cabinet. Then he closes it resolutely.

He faces us and lifts his eyebrows like it's our move now. Our time to move. To move out of his office. We don't.

'May I suggest a fundraiser, then. A cake stall. No, they don't do that anymore, I know. You're right. Something else. A table tennis tournament? No. You probably know what will work best in your town. Why don't you think about it.'

Wednesday 8.30am

'Why didn't you bloody suggest that in the first place? What do ya think I'm paying you for?' Finney is jiggling his tea bag like a madman and throws the sodden wad into the bin. The white flap doesn't open to receive it though, so it just slides down and onto the floor. I get up and put it in, wiping my hands on the tea towel afterwards.

'With all due respect Mr Finney,' says Fiona. She's wearing a black suit today. Stylish. Except for the white polka dots all over it. 'We've spent two thousand dollars filming a TV commercial, another $500 screening it, had legal advice, designed a flyer, got it printed. And you're suggesting we should have organised a *cake stall*.'

'Well it makes sense, doesn't it. Who doesn't like a bit of cake?'

'A diabetic?' says Karl. God, he's a nonger. Hasn't he heard of saccharine. Or carcinogenic aspartame, everyone's favourite for diet battery acid soft drinks.

I suddenly realise the intricate design over his tie is little batmen.

Finney scrapes a chair out from the table and plonks into it.

'Food allergies aside, it'd bring us all together, wouldn't it?'

Boyd throws his pen onto the table and swivels his beer bulk to one side. 'Great idea, Mr Finney! Simplicity. It's a great place to start. How much money are we looking at raising? What's the damage?'

'Fifty thousand, at least.'

'Fifty thousand from a cake stall?' Fiona does that I've-smelt-a-fart look.

'It's a start!'

'Why kind of cakes would people buy for fifty thousand dollars?'

'Perhaps ones with illicit substances,' says Karl, deadpan.

My eyes roll involuntarily at Karl. No wonder he was a high school drop out. He's just an idiot.

Finney's lip twitches. He pouts. He blinks. The man's face is a sea bed of moving parts.

'Well...one wouldn't...make it...*obvious*.' When his face moves like that, it must mean that he's thinking.

'What did ya say the name of that band'o yours was, young Jason?'

'Um. It's the *Nuns Frightened By Change*, sir.'

'*Nuns Frightened By Change*, huh? He.' He almost chuckles. More like a smile with a hiccup at the same time. Finally. Someone almost chuckles at the name of our band. Especially neat coming from a person high up in the government. Gareth'll be stoked.

Finney gets up and walks to the door. His slow and his eyes look like they're in deep focus.

'Organise me a cake stall, people. You know what to do. The targets fifty gees.' Finney turns back to look at me. 'Get that band'o yours on board, son.' He winks at me. I feel a bit slimed, to tell the truth. A bit like an odd uncle has said something...odd to me.

Finney leaves and closes the door. Boyd swivels back around, intent on the surface of the table with all its splashes of Lipton and red pen marks.

'Well,' he slaps his hand lightly on it. 'You heard the man. Who are we gonna get for a big stash of pot. Anyone know?'

It was silent. No one was prepared to say anyone's name. Not for a second anyway.

Then, 'Monica.' Karl.

I have to second him, but feel bad. 'Monica.'

Fiona is just nodding. She pushes her teeth together and kind of smiles in a grimacing sort of way.

'I think that's where Stevie gets his from.' Stevie's her boyfriend.

'Monica it is then.' A smile and one more Boyd-slap for luck. Then he chuckles and rubs his hands together.

As always after victory, the basketball bullfrog trainers shovel their way on top of the table. They stink.

3pm
'Only because...' she sighs. A long drawn-out sigh and no one cares to hear the answer. We just want to get inside and have a look.

'Mr Finney has been very good to me. Pivotal, really. Pivotal. Life changing. And I would require a small commission to cover basic costs.'

'Monica,' Fiona steps closer and whispers, 'It's okay. You're amongst friends. We just need to raise fifty grand. Can we have a look see?'

Monica nods, turns and from the massive chain of keys around her neck and caftan, inserts one into the padlock and opens up the double garage doors at her property.

'Wait a moment, while I get the light.' Then she switches the lights on—a whole shopping mall of them.

The garage is like a cross between a nursery and DJs. It's one memory I won't be forgetting in a hurry.

This is not good, is all I remember Boyd saying as he walks between the aisles of the greenery and the fountains and the lights. His face is almost horrified. But kind of titillated as well.

This is not good. But after a minute he must have changed his tune. He swings toward Monica, grabs both of her shoulders and kisses her fair and square on the lips. A pash, really. Joy and repulsion in one.

'It's PERFECT!'

Friday a week later — 6pm
People have started arriving and the hot cakes are selling like, well, hot cakes.

'They sell themselves,' says Finney, stuffing another $15 muffin between his fat cheeks, hands flapping around.

'I'm lovin' it.' Finney walks off. 'Lovin' it!'

Gareth and Kev and I start up our set. We play covers. We start with Stairway. It's a classic. People love it, people hate it. But it makes them laugh, cry, dance. Most importantly, open their wallets.

In the corner is the black-and-white photo from 1973. Finney's in it, holding the trophy. Best Team. Best under twenties footy team in the shire. Benley came second that year. But half of Benley's here so they don't notice enough to care. When they found out Monica was catering and it was a cake stall with a twist, thanks to Shirley's nice little flyer, they came in droves.

And it appears they are stocking up the larder for later. At nine, the charity muggers come out in droves as well. All the buckets get passed around, full as a goog. The chuggers don't have to harass for it even. The coin is still getting spilled by the volunteers from the TAFE hospitality department into the Save Landula glass box. It's piled pretty high. So is everyone else.

At eleven, Finney takes the stage. He's got a new microphone ring. Right now I like it a lot. It's one of the most beautiful pieces of bling I've seen.

'Ladies and gentlemen of Landula and Benley. Tonight we've come togther. We're saving our shires by uniting. We are uniting in fun, friendship, and food. Thanks so much to Monica.'

I roll the drums; Kev smashes the cymbal.

'Thanks to gorgeous Monica Metherin and the Whole Damn Collective Shire that we are. We may live in different towns, but we live as one. A name just isn't a difference. This Bowlo, thanks to your generosity of spirit and willingness to have a good time for a good cause, isn't gonna go away. It'll live on. Just like the photos on the wall. Age shall not weary them. And when you think we've lost, think again. We haven't lost. We've won. We've won the lot, the loot, the whole shebang! We've won it, 'cause we've stuck together!'

Then we play another couple of tracks. It's like the Hordern Pavilion, right here. We play, we joke on mike, we stuff around. It's great for our confidence.

Gareth's getting over his Hep C. He's shaking in a good way now. We're all just shaking together. Doing what we know. Doing what we can. And, thank God, work experience is over. What a high note to leave on. What a ride. Can't wait for school on Monday. The autograph pen is ready. And the success ring, gold and chunky and totally deserved. I am a legend. A red faced, ginger noggin legend.

Notes on Contributors

Susan Adams, PhD is an Australian poet published in nine countries. She was awarded 'Commended' in the 2012 O'Donoghue International Poetry Competition (Ire), 'Highly Commended' in the Val Vallis Award 2012 (Au), and 'Highly Commended' in the Adrien Abbott Poetry Prize 2012 (Au). She has been read on ABC Radio National. Publications include *Quadrant*, *Westerly*, *Southerly*, *Eureka Street*, *Hecate*, *Ascent* (Ca), *Social Alternatives*, *Cordite*, *FourW*, *The Long Paddock*, *Australian Poetry*. She is short listed for the Axel Clarke inaugural Poetry Prize. Her first book *Beside Rivers* released by Island Press (2013) was awarded 'Commended' in the FAW Anne Elder National Literary Award. http://islandpress.tripod.com/ISLAND.htm.

Jeffrey Alfier is a winner of the Kithara Book Prize for his poetry collection, *Idyll for a Vanishing River* (Glass Lyre Press, 2013). He is also author of *The Wolf Yearling* (Silver Birch Press) and *Terminal Island: Los Angeles Poems* (Night Ballet Press, forthcoming).

Stuart Barnes's poetry has appeared widely in publications such as *Assaracus: A Journal of Gay Poetry*, *Going Down Swinging*, *Mascara Literary Review*, *Southerly*, and *Verity La*, and is represented in the anthologies *Short and Twisted 2010*, *Time with the Sky*, *The Night Road*, *fourW twenty-three*, and *fourW twenty-four*. He is poetry editor of *Tincture Journal*, and is currently working on *Blacking Out and other poems*. He tweets at @StuartABarnes.

Andrew Bifield is an award-winning writer whose fiction and poetry has previously appeared in journals including *Regime Magazine*, *Quadrant*, *Island*, *Coppertales* and *LiNQ*. He has also written about the intersection between the arts, culture and economics for publications such as *artsHub* and the *Daily Review*.

Ahimsa Timoteo Bodhrán is the author of *Antes y después del Bronx: Lenapehoking* and the editor of an international queer Indigenous issue of *Yellow Medicine Review: A Journal of Indigenous Literature, Art, and Thought*.

In Australia, his work appears in *antiTHESIS*, *Burley*, *dotdotdash*, *Etchings*, *Going Down Swinging*, *Idiom 23*, *Island*, *Kurungabaa*, *Otoliths*, *Rabbit*, *Regime*, *Sketch*, and *Windmills*.

Andrew Burke is an Australian poet who moved from Perth to Corowa, NSW, in 2012. His current titles include *One Hour Seeds Another* (out now from Walleah Press), *Undercover of Lightness: New & Selected Poems* (Walleah Press, Hobart, 2012), *QWERTY* (Mulla Mulla Press, Kalgoorlie, 2011), and *Shikibu Shuffle* in collaboration with Phil Hall (above / ground press, Ontario, 2012). He is represented in *The Best Australian Poems 2012*, ed John Tranter, (Black Inc., 2012). In his spare time, Burke is a talent scout for Regime on the eastern seaboard. Read his daily posts at hispirits.blogspot.com.

Ashley Capes is an Australian poet, novelist and teacher. He is also a big fan of Studio Ghibli films and loves haiku.

Libbie Chellew is a short fiction writer from Melbourne. Her stories appear in *Antipodes*, *Verity La*, *Going Down Swinging*, *The Suburban Review*, *Wet Ink* and *Voiceworks*. She tweets as @Libbiec.

Sue Clennell's poetry has been published in various anthologies, including *Best Australian Poems 2011*, and school text books. Her short play 'The Unknown' was performed in Sydney's Short & Sweet Summer Festival, 2012. Two poems from Sue's CD, 'The Van Gogh Cafe', may be found on youtube.

Robbie Coburn was born in June 1994 in Melbourne and lives in the rural district of Woodstock, Victoria. His first book-length collection of poetry *Rain Season* was published by Picaro Press in 2013. He is well into a second collection, titled *the other flesh*. A chapbook, *Before Bone and Viscera* was published by Rochford Street Press in 2014 and is available for purchase here: http://rochfordstreetpress.wordpress.com/rochford-street-press-titles/.

Melissah Comber is a journalist from Newcastle, NSW who is well on her way to becoming the Australian Liz Lemon.

Raven Current remains a mystery.

Jim Davis is a graduate of Knox College and an MFA candidate at Northwestern University. Jim lives, writes, and paints in Chicago, where he reads for

TriQuarterly and edits *North Chicago Review*. His work has received Pushcart Prize and Best of the Net nominations, and has appeared in *Seneca Review, Adirondack Review, The Midwest Quarterly*, and *Columbia College Literary Review*, among others. In addition to the arts, Jim is a teacher, coach, and international semi-professional football player.

Ivan de Monbrison was born in Paris, France, in 1969.

Colin Dodds grew up in Massachusetts and completed his education in New York City. He's the author of several novels, including *WINDFALL* and *The Last Bad Job*, which the late Norman Mailer touted as showing 'something that very few writers have; a species of inner talent that owes very little to other people.' Dodds' screenplay, *Refreshment*, was named a semi-finalist in 2010 American Zoetrope Contest. His poetry has appeared in more than a hundred publications, and has been nominated for the Pushcart Prize. He lives in Brooklyn, New York, with his wife Samantha. You can find more of his work at thecolindodds.com.

Á. N. Dvořák is the illegitimate great-great-grandchild of the renowned Bohemian composer. Unlike his famous ancestor, he despises Wagner and his eyes more or less point in the same direction.

Phillip A. Ellis is a critic, poet and scholar. His work includes *The Flayed Man, Symptoms Positive and Negative, Arkham Monologues,* and *Four Ballades on the Crawling Chaos*. He edits *Melaleuca*, studies community services, and lives near Tweed Heads. His website is http://www.phillipaellis.com/

Aaron Furnell is just a young buck from SA's West Coast making his way in the Big Smoke of Adelaide, frivolously floating on the king tide of life.

Mike Greenacre is a Western Australian poet who has two published collections of poetry: *Kimberley Man* (2002) and *Beacon Breaker* (2010). He is a teacher who has taught in the Kimberleys and Goldfields before teaching in Perth schools. Some of his students have won prizes in The Young Writers' Contest. Mike is married to Tracy and has two adult children, Jonathan and Jaime.

Stu Hatton is a Melbourne-based poet and editor. He works in mental health research at the University of Melbourne. His poems have appeared in *The Age, Best Australian Poems 2012, Cordite Poetry Review, Overland,* and elsewhere.

His books are available from http://www.lulu.com/spotlight/stuhatton.

Kenneth Hudson is published in national and international journals, e-zines and anthologies.

Ross Jackson is a retired teacher who has had poetry and short stories published locally, interstate and in New Zealand. He is a regular reader at *Voicebox* in Fremantle.

Helga Jermy was born in the UK, migrating to Tasmania 20 years ago. Her poems have been published in various journals, anthologies and online, including *Regime, Rabbit Journal, Sotto, Flood Fire Famine*, and *A Hundred Gourds*. She is winner of Australian Poetry's poem of the year award for best of poems of the week.

Vasiliki Katsarou was born and raised in Massachusetts to Greek-born parents, and educated at Harvard College, the University of Paris I-Sorbonne, and Boston University. She is a Pushcart Prize-nominated poet whose poems have appeared in *Poetry Daily, wicked alice, Press 1*, and *US 1 Worksheets*, as well as in two upcoming anthologies: *Rabbit Ears: TV Poems* (Poets Wear Prada), and *Not Somewhere Else But Here: A Contemporary Anthology of Women and Place* (Sundress Publications). She has also worked in film and television production in France and Greece, and written and directed an award-winning 35mm short film, *Fruitlands 1843*, about the Transcendentalist utopian community. She currently directs the Panoply Books Reading Series in Lambertville, New Jersey.

Winifred Kavalieris — an Australian who has lived in New Zealand for 25 years.This means I'm also very much a Kiwi! I am inspired by Earth's wild places and the wild places of the human mind. Both Earth and Mind are awful, mysterious and delightful.

Christopher Konrad is a Western Australian writer. He has co-authored a recent book of poetry with two other WA poets, *Sandfire* (2011) published by Sunline Press and has poems and short stories published in many journals and on line. Along with other awards he received First Prize in the Tom Collins Poetry Award (2009), Creatrix Prize (2009), Spilt Ink Poetry Award (2012) and the Todhunter Literary Award (2012) for his short story 'The Soldier's Wife'. He completed his PhD in creative writing (2012) at Edith Cowan University. He currently teaches social sciences in Melbourne.

Roland Leach has three collections of poetry, the latest *My Father's Pigs* published by Picaro Press. He is currently the Poetry Editorial Advisor at UWA for *Westerly* and is proprietor of Sunline Press.

Cameron Lowe lives in Geelong. His third poetry collection, *Circle Work*, was published by Puncher & Wattmann in 2013.

Pushcart-nominee **Bruce McRae** is a Canadian musician with over 800 publications, including *Poetry.com* and *The North American Review*. His first book, *The So-Called Sonnets* is available from the Silenced Press website or via Amazon books. To hear his music and view more poems visit his website: www.bpmcrae.com, or TheBruceMcRaeChannel on Youtube.

Dean Meredith. Writer, voyeur, weirdo.

An eight-time Pushcart-Prize nominee and National Park Artist-in-Residence, **Karla Linn Merrifield** has had some 400 poems appear in dozens of publications. She has ten books to her credit; the newest are *Lithic Scatter and Other Poems* (Mercury Heartlink) and *Attaining Canopy: Amazon Poems* (FootHills Publishing). Her *Godwit: Poems of Canada* (FootHills) received the 2009 Eiseman Award for Poetry and she recently received the Dr. Sherwin Howard Award for the best poetry published in Weber - The Contemporary West in 2012. She is assistant editor and poetry book reviewer for *The Centrifugal Eye* (www.centrifugaleye.com). Visit her Vagabond Poet blog at http://karlalinn.blogspot.com.

Carly-Jay Metcalfe is a Brisbane-based death midwife in training. When she's not studying palliative care, she writes poetry, literary fiction, and memoir. She has plans to do her Masters in Spiritual Care next year and blogs at www.bruisesyoucantouch.com about life and most importantly, death.

Jan Napier lives near the Indian Ocean. her work has been published in *Westerly*, *Famous Reporter*, *Regime*, plus other journals and anthologies both here and overseas.

Allan Padgett has written poetry on and off ever since he was an angst-ridden teenager in country Victoria in the 60s (yes, he remembers — and was there). Now that he has grown up and retired, he has found the time and inspiration to write regularly. Reading regularly at Perth Poetry Club over the past four-five years has demonstrated to him the enormous value of 'the spoken word', and how reading poetry aloud to an audience, brings a poem to life and amplifies its meaning. Allan has worked in senior roles over 15 years with the Indigenous Land Corporation (WA State Manager) and the National Native Title Tribunal, and prior to all that, four years in national park joint management with the former Department of Conservation and Land Management. Prior to heading west 25 years ago to do a masters degree in natural resource management at UWA, Allan was Head of Applied Science and taught biology at Bendigo Regional College of TAFE. Allan comes from a dairy farming background, and lived for four wonderful and productive years on a hobby farm outside Bendigo where he and Jan raised four great kids and a menagerie of beasts — including geese, pigeons, donkey, cow, goats, ducks, Murray Cod, chooks, sheep, and old-fashioned roses and a cornucopia of edible plants. For eight of the past nine years, Allan retreated weekly from suburban Bedford in Perth to a 25 acre block at Toodyay for rest and recreation — and composing verse! (this Block de Paradise was sold at the end of 2012).

Geoff Page is based in Canberra and has published twenty-one collections of poetry as well as two novels and five verse novels. He's also won the Grace Leven Prize and the Patrick White Literary Award, among others. His recent books include *A Sudden Sentence in the Air: Jazz Poems* (Extempore 2011), *Coda for Shirley* (Interactive Press 2011), *Cloudy Nouns* (Picaro Press 2012), *1953* (University of Queensland Press 2013), *Improving the News* (Pitt Street Poetry 2013) and *New Selected Poems* (Puncher & Wattmann 2013). His *Aficionado: A Jazz Memoir* is forthcoming from Picaro Press.

Vanessa Page is a Cashmere poet who hails from Toowoomba in Queensland. She has published two collections of poetry — *Feeding Paper Tigers* (ALS Press, 2012) and *Confessional Box* (Walleah Press, 2013). She has twice been runner-up in the Arts Queensland Thomas Shapcott Poetry Prize.

Carl 'Papa' Palmer, retired Army, retired FAA, now just plain retired, lives in University Place, WA. He has seven chapbooks and a contest winning poem riding a bus somewhere in Seattle. Motto: Long Weekends Forever.

Richard King Perkins II is a state-sponsored advocate for residents in long-term care facilities. I have a wife, Vickie and a daughter, Sage. My work has appeared in hundreds of publications including *Poetry Salzburg Review, Bluestem, Sheepshead Review, Sierra Nevada Review, The William and Mary Review, Two*

Thirds North and *The Red Cedar Review*. I am a three-time Pushcart nominee and have work forthcoming in *Broad River Review*, *Emrys Journal*, *December Magazine* and *The Louisiana Review*.

Stephen Pollock is originally from Glasgow in Scotland. In 2009 he moved to Australia, where he works as a print journalist. He has had three short stories published, including two in the literary journal *Cracked Eye*. In 2013 he won the Darker Times Fiction competition and has had poetry published in the *Brisbane Speed Poets* journal. Most of his fiction is inspired by his former life in Glasgow, a city that throbs with drama and humour. He enjoys Vladimir Nabokov's novels and the poetry of Sylvia Plath and Ted Hughes.

Mark Roberts is a Sydney based writer and critic. He currently edits *Rochford Street Review*, *P76 magazine* and is poetry editor for *Social Alternatives* journal.

Mather Schneider – I am a 44 year old cab driver living in Tucson. I have been published in the small press for many years and have three full length books available on Amazon.

Michele Seminara is a poet from Sydney. Her writing has appeared in publications such as *Bluepepper*, *Tincture Journal*, *ETZ*, and *PASH Capsule*. She is also a yoga and meditation teacher with a passion for emptiness (the Buddhist kind). You can find her on twitter @SeminaraMichele.

Deborah Sheldon's short stories have appeared in many literary journals such as *Quadrant*, *Island*, *Crime Factory*, *Page Seventeen*, *Tincture Journal*, and *[untitled]*. Her fiction is also found in various anthologies including *Hard Labour* and *The One That Got Away*. Other fiction credits include the collection, *300 Degree Days and other stories*, and the crime-noir novella, *Ronnie and Rita*. She has another short story collection and two novels coming out over the next two years. Additional writing credits include commercial television scripts; stage and radio plays; magazine articles; award-winning medical writing; and non-fiction books for Reed Books and Random House. Deb lives in Melbourne, Australia.

Barnaby Smith's poetry has featured in publications in both Australia and the UK, including *Best Australian Poems 2012*, *Southerly*, *Cordite* and *Spineless Wonders*' 2013 anthology. He is also a music and arts journalist for *Rolling Stone*, *ABC Arts* and *The Quietus* and is one half of music duo *Telegraph Tower*.

Ian C Smith's work has appeared in *The Best Australian Poetry, London Grip, New Contrast, Poetry Salzburg Review, Quarterly Literary Review Singapore, The Weekend Australian,* and *Westerly*. His latest book is *Here Where I Work*, Ginninderra Press (Adelaide). He lives in the Gippsland Lakes area of Victoria, Australia.

Danielle Spinks is a Sydney-based writer and designer. Her writing has appeared in *HighLife Magazine, SOHI, Bewildering Stories,* Newcastle University's *Opus* and fiction anthologies, and various ghost blogs under other people's names.

Ashleigh Synnott — I am an emerging writer living and working in Sydney. I have had fiction published in various editions of the UTS Writers' Anthology. I have had non-fiction published in *Metro Film Magazine* and on *Concrete Playground* (Sydney, Melbourne, Brisbane and Auckland).

Roger Vickery is a Sydney writer. He has won several awards for fiction and poetry and his work has been published in anthologies, literary magazines, websites and newspapers in Australia and overseas. In 2013 he won the national Ned Kelly Crime Short Story Prize and the Bruce Dawe Poetry Award.

Ben Walter is a Tasmanian writer whose work has appeared in *Overland, Island, Griffith Review, Kill Your Darlings* and a range of other journals. His debut poetry manuscript, *Lurching*, was shortlisted in the 2013 Tasmanian Literary Prizes.

Printed in Australia
AUOC02n0737170714
262197AU00003B/3/P